Can We Save America?

The End of a Great Nation

By Steve Preston

1st Edition

Contents

Can We Save America? 1
Introduction 5
1st Constitution [1774] 15
    Elimination of Micro-colonies and Slavery 19
2nd Constitution 1781 22
3rd Constitution 1789 32
Slavery is Destroying our Country 36
Fix Our Schools 41
No Child Left Behind Disaster 45
Expansion of Deviant Sex 53
Re-read the First Amendment 70
    Increasing Moral Direction wil Reduce Drug use 92
Eliminate Slavery 96
    Cavanaugh on Irish Slaves 98
    Black Slavery 104
    Yellow Slaves 108
    Red Slaves 113
    Establish Jobs not Slavery 121
Control Workforce Expansion 131
Bring Back Families 143
    Stronger Families Reduce Crime 144
    Don't Glorify Baby Killing 145
Second Amendment 148
Understand the Ninth Amendment 151
Can We have Communism and Freedom? 154
Loss of the Tenth Amendment 157
    What About Controlling Federal Land? 158
    What About State Equality 160
    Statettes Versus States 164
Control Greed 171
    Strange Republic Conversion 173
    Labor Participation Rate 176
Democracy and Greed 179
Controlled Republic 182
    Oligopolies 184
Medical Greed Without Competition 187

College Greed Without Competition 195
Bring Back Americanism 197
   No American Pride 198
   Early Americanism/ Christianism 202
Promote General Welfare 206
Final Word.. 209

Introduction

Unbelievably our nation was founded on principles never tried before. Rather than establishing laws to protect a government or king, this one would be set up to care for the rights of the majority. There would be sacrifices to assure that liberty would allow for freedoms. Some try to put liberty and freedom on the same level but our founding fathers knew the difference and with some unseen guidance, they were able to establish the working Constitution that we have today. Since that time, our country has been almost destroyed by taking "control" away from the majority and giving it to the few again. I know that sounds like I'm pounding the rich, and I am, but that is only part of it. One of the real issues in America is the coddling of splinter groups and cults without consideration for the majority. Let's take for instance someone has a disease that no one else has. The man cannot afford payment to treat the disease and it is hugely expensive. What should the government do? Another similar idea is the allowance of snake worshiping by taking away rights of the Christian majority. In know someone is saying helping the sick man or religious tolerance is more important than building a country around the majority, but they are simply wrong and our Constitution was built around these very hard choices. What we will find is that each and every time this is done; our society slips farther and farther into a hole. Soon we will not be able to recover. Possibly that time has already passed, but I think there are things we can do to slow and even repair damage to our country before we go bankrupt like Greece, or have religious anarchy that seems to be happening in France, our we end with a level of debauchery that sickens the hardiest as was done in Rome.

I cannot assure you that everything in this book will be something you like, in fact, I'm sure Republicans, Democrats, Communists, and all the rest will get mad at one thing or another, but many of the things are things you need to hear and act on. Generally speaking the book is about small elements of the Constitution that are being ignored and abused to a level that is causing our country to fail. Don't get me wrong, there have been plenty of mistakes in our country and some of them were initially identified as important only to be reviewed later {by the majority} and found to be inappropriate. We will look at some of those, but here are the major elements of the Constitution and this book that can save us.

- *A requirement for the General Welfare*
- *A requirement for the Pursuit of Liberty*
- *A requirement of small federal government governing specific areas to protect the States*
- *A requirement to control greed without limiting growth*
- *A requirement to promote a civil family union.*
- *The amended requirement to assure "religious" freedom.*
- *The amended requirement to eliminate Slavery.*

It should be noted that the first 2 were so important they were stated over and over in all three of our Constitutions. It tells us something special about how the government will be run. Our 1st Constitution [1774] said stated it in a roundabout way.

> *To obtain redress which threaten destruction to the lives, liberty, and property of -subjects in North America- and the rights of freemen as inimical to the liberties of their country under the sacred ties of virtue, honor and love of our country*

Our Declaration of Independence [1776] said it more clearly as we began to understand the costs of both general welfare and liberty.

> *Life, Liberty, and the Pursuit of Happiness were sacred and it was the duty of the government, to provide new guards for their future security.*

Our 2nd Constitution [1781] said it this way.

> *The said "United States of America" enters into a firm league for their common defense, the security of their liberties, and their mutual and general welfare, binding themselves to assist each other, against all force offered, on account of religion, sovereignty, trade, or any other pretense whatever.*

Our last and current Constitution of [1787] was even more emphatic. The main topic throughout the document is a seemingly simple requirement.

> *"To promote the General Welfare, and secure the Blessings of Liberty to ourselves and our Posterity".*

This same sentiment was rooted in the founding fathers documents from the very first "Union of Colonies", so we can be sure that they believed these [General Welfare and Liberty] were of upmost importance and we will see how the elimination of these 2 founding father sentiments are helping to destroy our country. While these ideals are paramount in establishing a long lasting country, they are by no means the only areas where our Constitution has been trampled on to put money in the pockets of one group or another, or to pander some group by trampling on the rights of the majority, or to allow the festering of immorality or loss of country pride, or to establish poverty slaves that have continued to stack up issue after issue towards the final destruction of our country. We will see that a substantial amount deals with the pursuit of liberty and provision of general welfare of our citizens. Hopefully, we can begin to turn things around enough to limit its destruction.

Have we Lost Our Moral Compass?

The next 2 charts show one of the culprits. The Christian moral base of America is eroding. While Judeo-Christian religions have decreased by over 15% since 1950, other quasi-religious and cults have spreading non-Christian anything goes beliefs that are beginning to crack our countries foundation [Data from Gallop Poll].

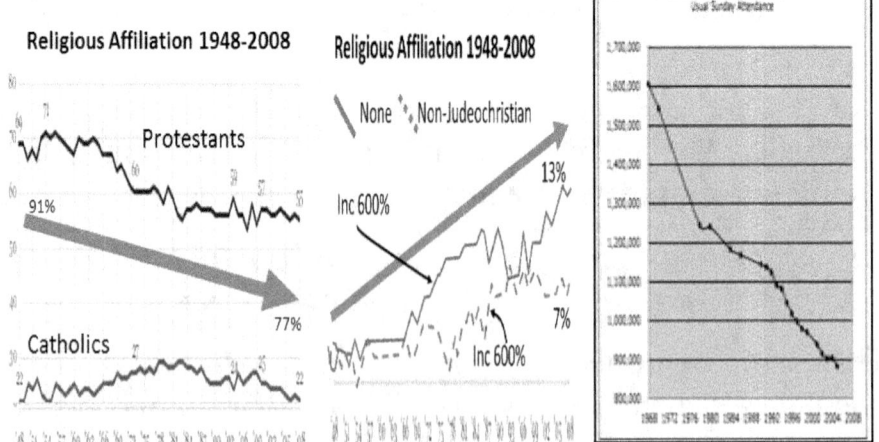

We will talk about that as we go along, but that isn't the whole picture. The last graph right shows a 50% drop in church attendance between 1969 and 2008. It seems as the number of citizens stop focusing on any moral compass the worse the country is. If the chart was extended it would show the slope did not start in 1968.

Is Unrestricted Immigration Dangerous?

I know this concept seems counter-intuitive, doesn't it? One might believe the easier we are on ourselves as Christians by not worrying about living up to fairly high moral standards the happier our nation will be. Unfortunately we become increasingly debased in what we as a nation ALLOW morally. Could it be that as Christian morality veers further and further from its steadfast adherence to the primary source of God's written Word, Christian morality becomes LESS relevant to America's success? I don't mean to sound preachy but it's the morality that is important here. We will examine some findings that may help us understand massive issues and concerns in this area.

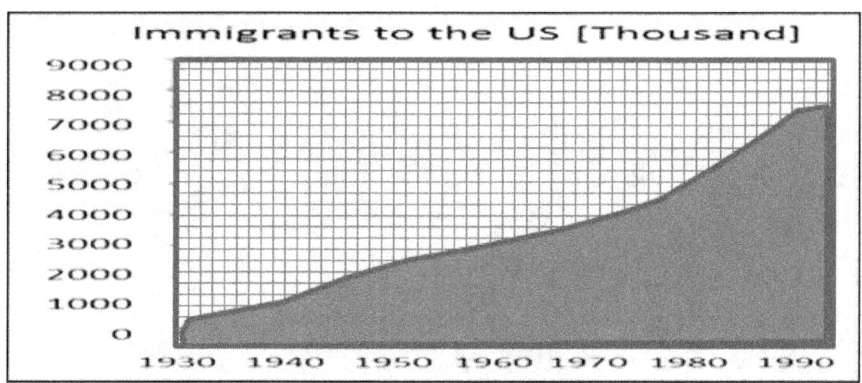

We can see from the last graph above that from 1930 until 1990 there has been a huge increase in immigration and that correlation of the new expansion in immigration tracks our country's slide into disaster. This doesn't mean a huge increase in immigration caused our issues by themselves, but it is a contributing factor we should discuss as a huge influx of cultists are arriving that could be dangerous. Unfortunately, the chart is not the whole story as we learn that there are 20 million "illegal" immigrants in the United State as well. We will look at them separately.

Destruction of Family is Pushing Disaster

Again let's begin by just looking at a simple graph. The graph to the left shows that the divorce rate has doubled since 1955, but that isn't the whole story. If we expand the graph [right we see the number of divorces have gone from about ½ million to over 20 million every year when we start in 1860. With no central home-life, wandering children use gangs and substitute families.

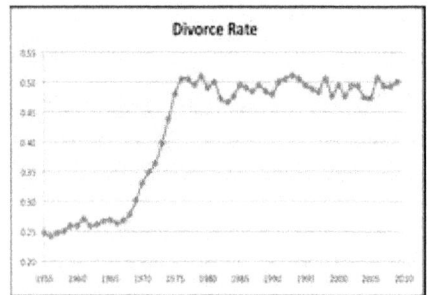
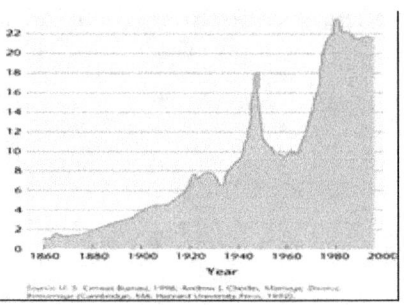

I know it looks like things were getting better after World War II until 1965. Just remember that date as we go along as it will make more sense.

Unmarried Families?-From the previous images, one might thing we have a large number of unwed families as the family erodes still further in America and loss of a family association has drastically changed how Americans work together to build America. The free spirit concept works for hippies, but not when we are in crisis mode as our country is faltering.

Without supervision this is a tragedy waiting to happen. There are ways to deal with this growing issue that will be discussed.

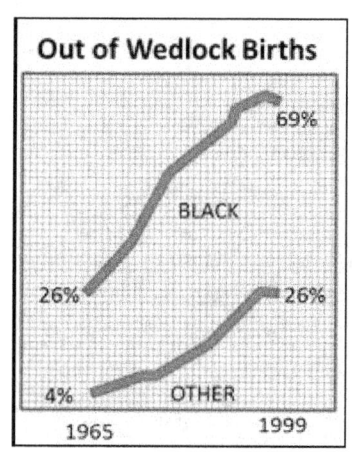

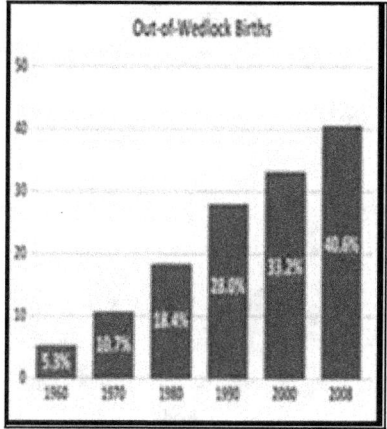

Incarcerations Swamping our Country

With no hope, more and more are turning to crime as shown below. Without prospect of a job, criminals are flourishing and there seems to be no end as fewer and fewer jobs are available, people are becoming less and less skilled, and they have less drive than ever before. This also can be turned around. The following graph shows this horrible trend. From 1910 until 2000 the number has increased by 1400% with the fastest slope starting about 1965.

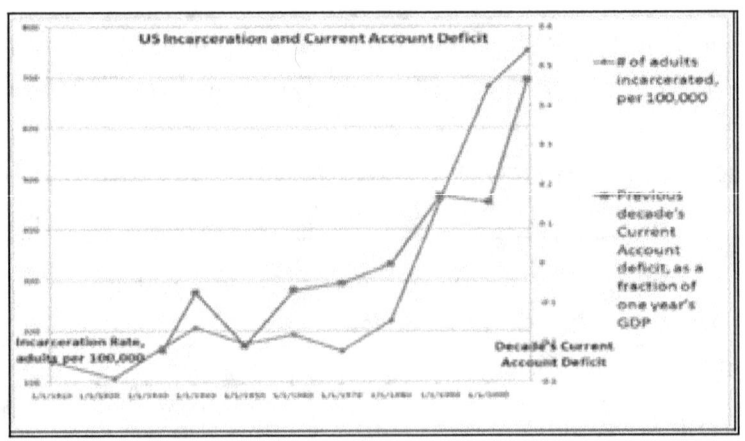

Killing Babies

The loss of family life is no more evident as in the statistics of birth control by killing. While abortion is a nice name for a horrible act, it in no way reduces the problems in our society associated with what is driving the rise in the number of abortions from 1973 to 2008 to be well over 5 ½ million under what is laughingly called "Planned Parenthood". [See below]

Planned Parenthood "eliminates parenthood".

If you think this disregard for life and parenthood is part of the cause for the demise of America you might be on to something. By the way, I was not laughing when I wrote Planned Parenthood. While the concept has a feeling of help, its mission has been changed from trying to support parenthood to just killing an aggravation. Its very essence is to reduce the moral character of our nation. It teaches Americans they are not responsible even for bringing life into our land.

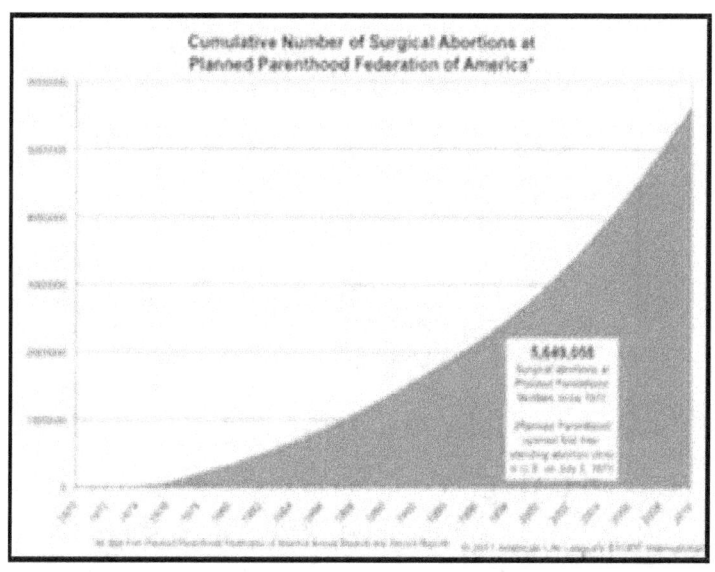

Cumulative Number of Surgical Abortions at Planned Parenthood Federation of America

5,649,058

Destruction of Schools is Killing America

Early in our existence, our country had one of the top school systems in the world, Ranked 1st in many of the tested areas, our schools produced some of the top scientists, engineers and thinkers to expand our prosperity, but around 1965, everything started a downward turn. Things like slipping standards, a program called "No Child Left Behind", shaming normalcy, eliminating God and making sex more exciting all are helping to dumb our children and make an atmosphere that is not conducive to learning. There is no reason we should not be able to regain our rightful place in the world concerning schools, but as we look around we will surely get depressed. Our children are not gaining the skills necessary to build our country strong. The next graph shows that while women are increasing training in colleges, the men of our country are losing site of how to survive at an alarming rate.

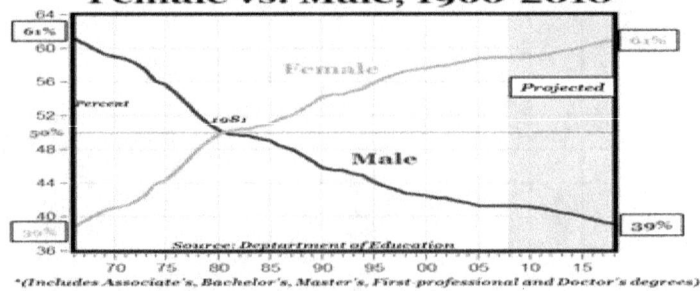

Percent of All College Degrees*
Female vs. Male, 1966-2018

64
61%
60
Female
56
Projected
Percent
52
1981
50%
48
Male
44
40
39%
36
70   75   80   85   90   95   00   05   10   15
*(Includes Associate's, Bachelor's, Master's, First professional and Doctor's degrees)

Source: Deptartment of Education

Greed Has Made a Mockery of America

For this we need to go back to what was laughingly called our 4th Civil War in 1862. As we look at the causes of the internal war, greed describes the failures. Over 80 percent of the richest men EVER in the United States made their money off the 600 thousand dead soldiers of the made up war. Afterwards, the United States was almost turned into a single factory controlling everything in America. We had turned into a Fascist State with about 30 rulers. Even the presidents bowed to their ways. We may never know what happened, but in the mid to late 1870s things changed and it saved our country. We need to see what happened and also see what we can do today to control greed without stifling growth or we will succumb to disaster.

So we have a dilemma. If we try to control the rich, we turn into a greed filled democracy and Fascist state. IF we increase poverty slaves and help the minority over the majority we become a socialist/communist state. We will not survive either one. Before we can understand how to save our country we must first look at how we got our 3rd Constitution so we can understand what it says as it can help us clear up a lot of this mess just be doing what was laid out for us.

1st Constitution [1774]

The United Colonies simply worked as a band of separate interests for a time, as the King of England pushed us to the limit. It would not be until the 2nd Colonial Congress came into being under President Peyton Randolph that we would finally adopt a Constitution. Ruggles, our first American President, had gone into hiding because of his treasonous actions in not even signing our first Declaration of Independence by this time. President Peyton was a true leader and the Union of American Colonists began to take steps to understand what **General Welfare** and the **Pursuit of Liberty** would be for them. He would run our country and adopt our first Constitution called the **Articles of Association.** This Constitution was somewhat limited in scope for governing beyond the elimination of slavery, the halting the purchase of tea, and limitations concerning how many pimentos one was allowed to eat, but it certainly was a start to show the cost of freedom and general welfare. I'm just being critical about the pimentos, as it was a good start. There would be a level of suffering that would allow these things to happen and the Congress and our President knew it. The people knew it and set up rules and processes to achieve them. The following image is a complete copy of our first Constitution.

It was President Randolph's time to be famous. Ten years had passed since our first President's treachery, the British were even more oppressive than they had been before the first Declaration of Independence, and the population was more strongly convinced that there was a price to pay for **general welfare** and the **pursuit of liberty**. No one was going to get a free lunch, no one was going to be given special consideration and all had to participate or they would be shunned by those fighting for a continuation of general welfare. This was becoming a democratic environment with all citizens having to take part or leave. While the Constitution they established was fairly loose in design, our President proudly signed the document putting a target on his head along with others in the Congress. Even at this early date in 1774, there was not only a strong feeling for promoting the General Welfare and Freedom, there was also a strong desire to expand our United Colonies from the current 11 colonies. The desired goal included a split of Pennsylvania into the religious sector and a more liberal section now called Delaware who wanted to keep slavery and drinking alive, Georgia who was finally coming on board, Canada who had been asked to join the United Colonies over the last ten years, and the simple takeover of all the land called <u>Vandalia</u> that had been given to the Indians against the wishes of the colonists. They hated the Indians and would refer to them as savages in the new Constitution. By declaration our country would be doubled in size even with Canada rejecting the invitation and Americans would learn what **promoting the General Welfare and Freedom would cost us dearly**. The image following shows our original united colonies and the size we represented in our second Declaration of Independence after taking control of Vandalia. Our newest additions were New Hampshire, Georgia, and the colony of Vandalia that was split among the various colonies.

A Crazy Constitution

This would be a crazy constitution. After our first "Declaration of Independence" [Declaration of Rights and Grievances]" this first Constitution would change the colonies into a nation with the rights and duties of a nation. Let's review this important document to compare characteristics with our 3rd Constitution we are using now so we can better understand who our Constitution can save us if we let it. Certainly, there was a flavor of British rule acceptance, but we can tell the union was now thinking like a separate country.

But just what did our first Constitution say?

It starts off innocuous enough with praise to our big brother Britain and sort of vowing allegiance only to turn around and begin an attack on the oppression, the enslavement, and the ruinous nature of the British rule--- to go along with the Declaration of Independence that had been sent.

Praise and Anguish Section [Paraphrased]

We, his majesty's *most loyal subjects, the delegates of the several colonies of New Hampshire, Massachusetts Bay, Rhode Island, Connecticut, New York, New Jersey, Pennsylvania, the three lower counties of New Castle, Kent and Sussex, on Delaware, Maryland, Virginia, North Carolina, and South Carolina, deputed to represent them in a continental Congress-- are oppressed; -- occasioned by a ruinous system of colony administration, -- calculated for enslaving these colonies,*

Please notice Georgia was excluded in the original colonies of the union.

Trade Refusal Section

In North America, we are of opinion, that a non-importation, non-consumption, and non-exportation agreement, will prove the most effectual as follows:
- *Article 1- Law against buying Pimento*
- *Article 2- Law against buying slaves*
- *Article 3- Law to halt drinking of Tea*
- *Article 4- Law to delay constitutional action*
- *Article 5- Law against foreign Merchant Piracy*

- *Article 6- Law against domestic Merchant Piracy*
- *Article 7- Law to produce domestic sheep*
- *Article 8- Law against wearing Scarves at funerals*
- *Article 9- Law against price gouging*
- *Article 10- Establishment of Welfare for Bostonians*
- *Article 11- Law against Treason*
- *Article 12- Law of Inspection*
- *Article 13- Price Control Law*
- *Article 12- Federal control over inter-colony trade and commerce*

Call for the Repeal Section

- *No trial by jury was made illegal*
- *Law against blocking Boston harbor was established*
- *Law against altering the Boston charter was established*
- *Law to extend the limits of Quebec was allowed*

While one would think the book would discuss the welfare of the Bostonians clause, but what we will look at a little later is the discussion about freeing the slaves and how it affected the General Welfare described in the 3rd Constitution we use now. First we need to get into a war. Soon the country was at war in the area known as Vandalia and then it expanded to all the united colonies.

Elimination of Micro-colonies and Slavery

General welfare would require similar say in our government. The early founding fathers knew of the issues of the micro-colonies and how their representation in Congress was substantially more that the "normal sized" States, so there was a campaign. Some may not have been told this in school, but I think it is important. While Rhode Island, Connecticut, Delaware, and New Hampshire were split into micro-States again at a later time; during the time of the "Sons of Liberty" up until at least 1774, they were all piled into one colony and the flag had only 9 stripes representing North and South Carolina, Virginia, New York, New Jersey, Pennsylvania, Massachusetts [including Maine], and the **North East micro-colonies** [including Connecticut, Delaware, Rhode Island, New Hampshire] as shown below. Many knew we could not establish equal opportunity of each State with Rhode Island being considered a State. It should be noted that the increased representation of the tiny New England Statettes was a major reason for most of the Civil Wars including the one in 1862.

Their snake flag went even farther making a reasonable State by adding Massachusetts to the North East micro-colony set. The "Sons of Liberty" warned that if the Colonies did not join together they would soon die, as shown on the snake flag to the left. I guess the fear tactics worked as we soon would declare our Independence in a more strong way. They also warned of consolidation or unrest would be certain. This warning went unanswered. One of the campaign warnings of these courageous people beginning to fill the groundwork for our Constitution was to establish all Americans as individuals with all having liberty. Because of the massive conviction of John Jay who would soon become President and others, our new country would eliminate slavery. This attempt was focused mostly on indentured slaves of the North, but would soon be tried in the south where black slaves were becoming a major commodity. Let's look at the elimination of slavery article.

Article 2 Elimination of Slavery

We will neither import nor purchase, any slave imported after the first day of December next; after which time, we will wholly discontinue the slave trade, and will neither be concerned in it ourselves, nor will we hire our vessels, nor sell our commodities or manufactures to those who are concerned in it.

To many this stand against slavery sounds odd given the harsh words in our second Constitution and the details about slaves only being 3/5 of a person as identified in the 3rd and final Constitution, but there is a story to tell. We'll look at this some more as it helps us understand about our new form of slavery.

2nd Constitution 1781

The Congress changed its name from Colonial Congress to Continental Congress to show their separation more distinctly and they adopted our second Constitution called the "Articles of Confederation". One month after the battle of Lexington, our country founding fathers set up new orders, new requirements and a new President. This congressional government lasted the first 4 years of the Revolutionary War. There had been 2 Presidents under the Articles of Confederation and now it was time for a new President named John Hancock. Fifty six delegates from 12 colonies including the sort of colony/state of Delaware convened. Georgia was still missing and a more detailed Constitution was drafted. Here is the gist of the 2nd Constitution.

Strengths over the Previous Constitution

The Strengths of this new Constitution over the Articles of Association include the following: [Some might say, today that being able to make money willy-nilly was not necessarily strength but here are commonly accepted ones.]

- *Federal Government could declare war and make peace.*
- *Federal Government could coin and borrow money*
- *Federal Government could sign treaties with foreign countries*
- *Federal Government could operate post offices*
- *States could determine Slavery Issues*

Weaknesses to be Resolved

Unfortunately, there were some weaknesses that showed up rather quickly as States began to squabble. These would be fixed in the 3rd Constitution.

- *Federal Government did not have the power to tax*
- *They had no power to enforce laws*
- *Congress lacked strong and steady leadership*
- *Our government had no national Army or Navy*
- *There was no system of national courts*
- *Each State could issue its own paper money*
- *States could put tariffs on trade between States.*

2nd Constitution and Slavery

As noted above the condemnation of slavery was removed in the 2nd Constitution and States could allow or not allow slavery as they wished. This new Constitution was called the "Articles of Confederation". [First page is shown next]

As time went on, someone said let's rename our congress again so they did. The **"Congress of the Confederation of the United States in Congress Assembled"** lasted from 1781 to 1789. The biggest thing to note besides the war being in full swing was they were trying to get rid of the Constitution and replace it with a new one that got rid of all the free the slave stuff. Initial meetings of the 2nd Congress established a wide assortment of changes. <u>This new Constitution would finally become the governing document from March 1, 1781, until the 3rd Constitution went into effect on March 4, 1789.</u> Here is a list of the Presidents that reigned prior to this major document. There were 10 presidents that served during our 2nd Constitution. George Washington became the 1st President after our 3rd Constitution. The Traitor President and six Presidents that served under the Articles of Association are shown below.

- **Timothy Ruggles -<u>First President</u>** during our <u>1st Declaration of Independence.</u> He can also be named the first Traitor President.

- **Peyton Randolph** 1774- **First President** after during our <u>1st Constitution</u>

- **Henry Middleton** 1775- **First President** to become prisoner of war

- **John Hancock** 1777- **First President** when <u>our 2nd Declaration of Independence</u> was drafted and first pirate President.

- **Henry Laurens** 1778- First Slave mogul President

- **John Jay_**1779- **First President** to initiate emancipation of Slaves and youngest Present EVER.

- **Samuel Huntington** 1780- First President during the 2nd Constitution **and possibly the first Slave President**.

Samuel Huntington

Samuel Huntington was our 7th President September 28, 1779 - July 9, 1781. He has a couple of unusual claims. He served as the last President under the 1st Constitution and he was reelected to become the first President under the 2 Constitution. He was that good!! I know we praise this guy a little too much but some of it was how he became President. While there is much confusion about this man, don't tell me a poor man can't become President. According to many, this guy had been enslaved and was dirt poor after he finally was set free during a time when not having money generally made you less than a person. I know Andrew Johnson is considered the first slave President identified by most, but Samuel Huntington may also have been an indentured slave according to one of the 4 substantially different histories. If he was brought over from Scotland to work the fields of the Governor of Connecticut he would have been our first slave President rather than Andrew Johnson. According to most histories, Samuel Huntington had no schooling, never quit learning on his own, and always pushed himself. This was the best self-made man President one could imagine. This guy was totally different that almost all Presidents in that he had a different perspective of "General Welfare and the Pursuit of Liberty for our Posterity." Let's look at several of the descriptions of this great American.

History #1 as a Field Slave-As an impoverished indentured servant from Scotland, his main job in America had been plowing the fields of a very popular and kind Governor of Connecticut, probably Roger Wolcott. I know you are wondering why a kind man would have slaves, but this was during a time when a substantial number of people owned this type of worker and hiring a man to do field work often would result in the man leaving to find freedom in the dead of night. Slavery was a way to assure a worker stayed. Anyway, Samuel Huntington didn't want to plow his entire life and he knew some reading and writing skills from before he had been enslaved. He was able to get books from his kind master and studied all the time. Finally, unlike most, his master did not continue his enslavement and Samuel was freed and became a lawyer; a good one. He was so good; he was considered one of the greatest self-made men among the founders as he had mastered law without school. He was also one of the greatest legal minds of the age. Then **he was elected twice as President of the United States**.

History #2 As an Indentured Cooper-Samuel Huntington was born on July 16, 1731 in Windham, Connecticut to a Puritan farmer. When Samuel was 16 he was indentured as an apprenticed to a cooper [someone who made barrels banded with copper], but somehow he continued to work on his father's farm. This one seems odd in that an indentured apprentice would not be working the farm simultaneously. His education came from books borrowed from local lawyers so Sam forsook the farm and forsook backing barrels and became a lawyer. In 1754 Samuel was admitted to the bar, and the rest is the same.

History #3 As a Wealthy Farmer-Samuel Huntington was born in Windham, Connecticut, to a worthy farmer. Several of his brothers devoted themselves to the gospel ministry as Calvinists. While his brothers went to seminary, Samuel had to Stay and run the farm and would not have a formal education as he was the oldest son. In the evenings, Sam would read continuously. The library of a respectable lawyer in a neighboring town, furnished him with the necessary law books which allowed him to become a lawyer.

What About Andrew Johnson?

While I'm on the Slave President theme, I might as well refresh details that should have been establishing in school as there is a level of honor being the first runaway slave President. For sure Andrew Johnson's slavery was much more intense as he was a hunted runaway slave before finally becoming President of the United States. Enslaved at age 10 as an indentured "servant/apprentice" to a tailor, he, his brother William and 2 others escaped from their master in 1824 when Andrew was when 16 and his brother was 21. A reward was set for their return with a special emphasis on Andrew as detailed below. Make no mistake; apprentice was just a bond servant or slave.

Notice of Runaway Apprentices

June 24, 1824

TEN DOLLARS REWARD.

Ran away from the Subscriber, on the night of the 15th instant, two apprentice boys, legally bound, named WILLIAM and ANDREW JOHNSON. The former is of a dark complexion, black hair, eyes, and habits. They are much of a height, about 5 feet 4 or 5 inches. The latter is very fleshy, freckled face, light hair, and fair complexion. They went off with two other apprentices advertised by Messrs. Wm. & Chas. Fowler. When they went away, they were well clad—blue cloth coats, light colored home-spun coats, and new hats, the maker's name in the crown of the hats, is Theodore Clark. I will pay the above Reward to any person who will deliver said apprentices to me in Raleigh, or I will give the above Reward for Andrew Johnson alone.

No telling what would have happened if he had been captured and sent back to his master. Instead, he hid and wandered and became the only southern Senator to stay with the Union. As Andrew was coming to Washington,

27

Virginians captured him as set up a noose for lynching. One courageous man claimed that the people of Tennessee had requested the lynching opportunity. As Andrew was from Tennessee they let him go, temporarily. Andrew got out of there and became a running mate with Lincoln who won the presidency. Andrew got drunk. When Lincoln was killed, this previous slave decided to heal the wounds of war and established simple rules. President issued a proclamation to the defeated Agrarian States.

If the previous States of rebellion end slavery and pledge loyalty to the USA they can send representatives to Congress.

That is exactly what they did and everything seemed fine as the southern congressmen arrived but the other congressmen, against the law, refused to allow the new congressmen their proper place. Naturally, Johnson was as outraged as the congressmen and the citizens of the States they represented.

Unbelievable Misdirection of the Constitution

You would think there would be something done. The sneaky Congress employed Lincoln's Secretary of War, Edwin Stanton, to begin putting burdens on the newly reentered States so Andrew Johnson fired him when he could take no more. Here is where it gets weird. Totally against the Constitution, they passed this bogus law that would not let Johnson fire any of his employees or appointments. Certainly, the Supreme Court indicated it was unconstitutional, but not before Johnson was impeached to end the first and only runaway slave President reign.

John Jay

Sorry for the diversion, but some have not even been taught about some of these Presidents and Andrew Johnson's beginning as a <u>runaway slave</u> should be proclaimed, not hidden. Another important founding father is President John Jay. He was our first President to really push emancipation of slaves and he was our youngest President ever at only 34. He was younger by far than either Teddy Roosevelt [42] or John Kennedy [43] who have both been acclaimed for youth. The main thing is he was the State's leading opponent of slavery. His first two attempts to pass laws for the emancipation of all slaves in New York failed in 1777, so he tried again in 1785. That failed also as New Yorkers loved having slaves. He then tried a third time in 1799 and slaves were free well after our 3rd Constitution came along. He also came up with the Manumission Society, in 1785. I know it's a stupid made up word, but it organized boycotts against newspapers and merchants in the slave trade and provided legal counsel for free black and white people claimed as slaves. Besides being a judge, it seems this slavery issue was his passion.

Presidents Under the New Constitution

The list below shows a new lot of Presidents that would try their hand at providing the <u>general welfare and pursuit of liberty</u> that will be so very important for our survival.

- **Thomas McKean** 1781- He was the **First President** after The British surrendered, but somehow we forget.

- **John Hanson** 1782- He was the **First President** after war officially ended and first under a new name "United States in Congress Assembled", but somehow we forget.

- **Elias Boudinot** 1783- He was the 10th President since the 1st Constitution.

29

- **Thomas Mifflin** 1784- He was the 11th and first Quaker President.

- **Richard Henry Lee** 1785- Lee was our 12th President and was to draft the Declaration of Independence, but sickness had his protégé' Jefferson do it with his help.

- **John Hancock** (again) 1786- While the old smuggler was elected again, he mostly got sick and turned power over to David Ramsey who did almost everything.

- **Nathaniel Gorham** 1786- This was our First President to have to serve during our 1st Civil War [Shay's Rebellion]

- **Arthur St. Clair** 1787- This was our 15th and last President allowed to be born outside the United States [He was born in Scotland]. I know Obama might be another exception, but we will never know.

- **Cyrus Griffin** 1788- Griffin was our 16th President or 9th under "Articles of Confederation." He also was the last president to serve under the 2nd Constitution.

- **George Washington** 1789-1797- This is the one we remember the most. He was **1st President after the 3rd Constitution**, 10th after the 2nd Constitution, and 17th after the 1st Constitution.

As President John Hanson signed the new treaty, our country and our mind set changed. The image below shows this great change. It would be another 8 years before a third Constitution would come about.

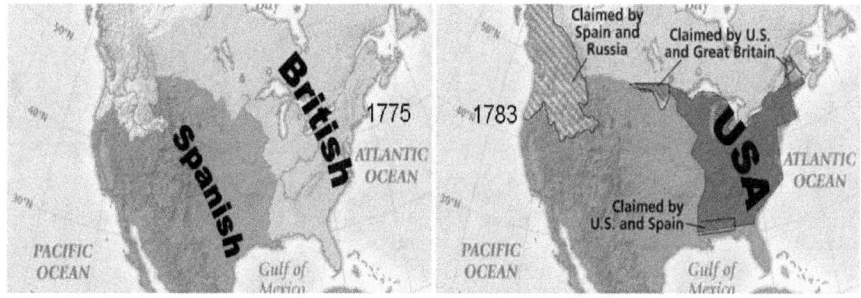

Our nation had gone through 2 Declaration of Indepenences and 3 Constitutions by the time of George Washington. Our first President is described on the following image along with some of the more colorful Presidents of that time.

Our First President

Timothy Ruggles
First President After the 1st Declaration of Independenc

Peyton Randolph
First President After the 1st Constitution

John Hancock
First President After the 2nd Declaration of Independence

John Jay
First and youngest Presiden Pushed Freedom of Slaves

Samuel Huntington
First President after 2nd Constitution[possibly slave]

Tom Mckean
First President after we won the Revolution

John Hanson
First President after Revolution Peace Treaty

Nathan Gorham
First President to encounte a Civil War

George Washington
First President after the 3rd Constitution

31

3rd Constitution 1789

Finally we get to the one everyone remembers and the one that is going to get us out of this mess if we let it. Some call it the Pro-Slavery Constitution. While the first 2 Constitutions eliminated or seemed to restricted Slavery, the one ratified during Cyrus Griffin's Presidential term in office not only seemed to encourage it, it placed specific characterizations about slaves not being "Real People". Here is an excerpt.

Article I- *"Representatives and direct taxes shall be appointed among the several States which may be included within this union, according to their respective numbers, which shall be determined by adding to the whole number of free persons* **[again indicating that non-free people were unacceptable or they would not provide the distinction]**, *including those bound to service for a term of years, and excluding Indians, not taxed,* ***three fifths of all persons.'*** Therefore slaves were not even considered a whole person in a census. A slave was only 3/5th of a person.

Article IV-*No person held in service or labor in one State, under the laws thereof, escaping to another, shall, in consequence of any law or regulation therein, be* *discharged from such service or labor, but shall be delivered up on claim of the party to whom such service or labor may be due.*

That's a long drawn out way of saying that if you find a slave; you must return him to his owner. After all they are only 3/5ths of a person. Make no mistake, it is not talking about prisoners held by a State it is talking about prisoners held by individuals. The direct indication that "ANY PARTY" could claim the "laborer held in servitude" allows an individual to own a person.

We the People of the United States, in Order to form a more perfect Union, establish Justice, insure domestic Tranquility, provide for the common defense, <u>promote the general Welfare,</u> and <u>secure the Blessings of Liberty to ourselves and our Posterity,</u> do ordain and establish this Constitution for the United States of America.

Form a More Perfect Union-This means that the rights of each person and each State would be made equal or as equal as possible and for religions not being hampered by the government as we learn later.

Establish Justice-This means the rights defined by a majority would be assured for all. While this did not include Indians or Slaves, there were provisions later to involve them as well.

Insure Domestic Tranquility-Elimination of Fear and strife.

Provide the <u>Common</u> Defense-Protection of our country controlled by a federally mandated Army and Navy. The following image shows the beginning of this great document that is so often misquote, abused, and trampled.

General Welfare and Secure Liberty

This last part of the preamble is the main part that has been sorely misquoted and abused. Welfare payments that are taxed if someone works are the exact opposite to welfare of a population like our United States. When the framers added the blessings of liberty it eliminated the giving of money without work. The idea we call those types of payments welfare is totally different than this passage is trying to establish. Instead to establishing liberty and GENERAL welfare, the payments tear down the very fiber of a democracy and our republic. There is no question those payments disrupt and tear down the general welfare of our country as we will see and they completely destroy the opportunity to secure the blessings of liberty. Liberty is a funny word. On one hand liberty is the opposite of promoting welfare, but on the other hand they go hand in hand. Many times the second half of the welfare statement is used for newspapers being allowed to print what they work for but there is more to that part of the preamble as well.

I know this sounds like some hard-hearted analysis driven by greed but it is not. We need to protect our poor and we need to protect all Americans. Sometimes we need to protect them from themselves. If you ever wondered why socialist and communist governments fail, it is the "joy of freedom part". In a communist government, people are pushed into a desperate need for the government to take care of them so all freedom is lost.

Freedom REQUIRES independence or independence REQUIRES work to allow for freedom.

A government that does not establish a limit on loss of independence will certainly fail and general welfare will be lost. It appears we are losing the welfare of the General population and our "protect our country" freedom with earned income credit, food stamps, free housing, free medical and all the rest. Luckily, there is a way back to reason. What is happening is a travesty and we are returning to Slavery in an awful way.

.

Slavery is Destroying our Country

Some of the areas we will touch include moral direction, immigration, family life and ideals, our failed schools, politics and corruption, greed and hate, and something called liberty or the elimination of "poverty slaves". This poverty slave thing might be the worst of the worst problem facing America today. This is not the same thing as elimination of poverty, so don't go thinking the way out of this mess is to simply giving people money. About 1954 an important truth was written into the Congressional Record that is important to this book.   Please read this over and over as you read through this book.

*"**You cannot legislate the poor into freedom** by legislating the wealthy out of freedom. The government cannot give anybody anything without first taking it away from somebody else. When ½ the people get the idea that they do not have to work because the other half is going to take care of them, and when the other half gets the idea that it does no good to work because somebody else is going to get what they work for, that my dear friends is about the end of any nation. You cannot multiply wealth by dividing it."*

Poverty Slaves- Between the 1630s and the American Revolution, one-half to <u>two-thirds of white immigrants to the American colonies arrived as slaves</u> called Indentured

Servants. Make no mistake these were slaves, treated like slaves, thrown away like slaves and bred like slaves.

*Only **about 40 percent of indentured servants lived** to complete the terms of their contracts. Female servants were often the subject of harassment from their masters. A woman who became pregnant while a servant often had years tacked on to the end of her service time.* These slaves are not what I'm talking about in this book so much; nor am I talking about the African slaves that followed or the Chinese enslaved railroad workers or the American Indian enslavement. I will provide a comparison, but what is killing America is "poverty slaves" who have lost their liberty as the government pays them to stay enslaved. The next chart showed that over 50% of Americans have significant handouts from the government for survival. To show how much the problems have expanded, the chart from Pennsylvania shows the number of <u>people on welfare programs for their living</u>. In 2011 1.25 people worked for every person living on welfare. Today it is even worse.

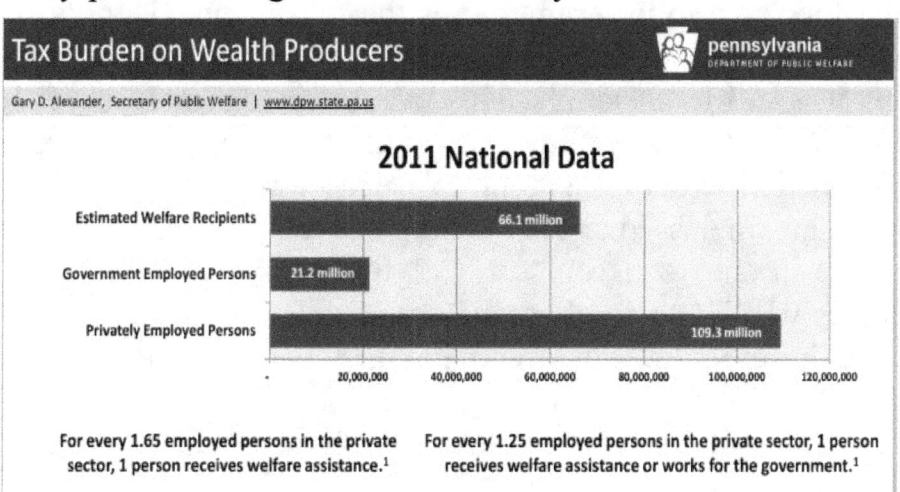

The chart following right shows the various areas of government assistance. Rather than consolidating the festering wound, these non-working welfare programs have been split into dozens of different named elements to make it not look as serious as it is. Possibly one thing we could do to help fight this epidemic is to consolidate the welfare programs so we can tell what is being done.

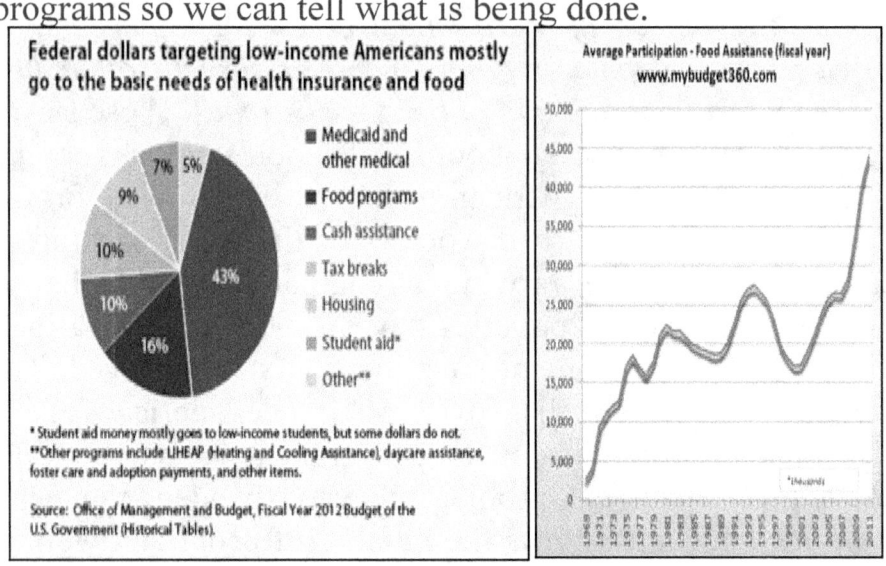

Food Stamps-As one of the symptoms of poverty slaves, the food Stamp program shows the expansion. I know we call it SNAP today to keep people from being embarrassed, but it is still food stamps. This spiral started around 1965. In by 1970 there were about 5 million on food assistance. Today the number has gone to 45 million, almost 10 times as many in less than 50 years. [See above right] By this chart, in the next 50 years all inhabitants of the United States will be on food assistance. Our standard of living is quickly eroding, our freedoms are being stolen as our general Welfare is eroding, the job markets are being reduced, and our children have little hope of finding liberty. We can do something about it, but we had better get started. I think the first place to start is in our schools.

The following chart shows the change in taxation from 1913 until about 2008. It looks like the rich pay about the same as everyone else, but it is very misleading.

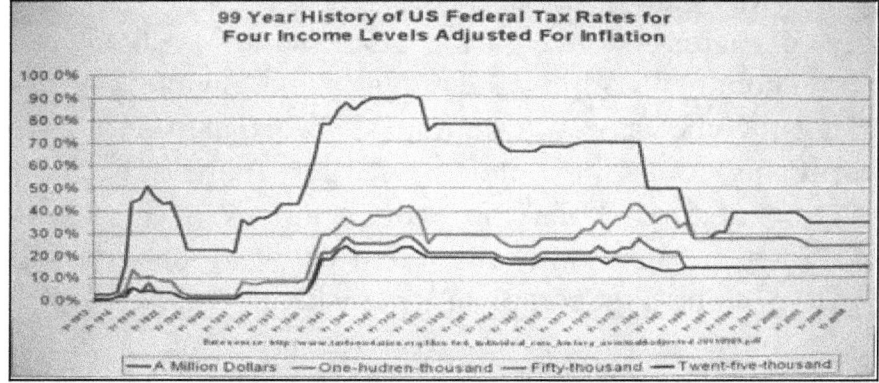

This is actually a lie in that the lowest group gets their money back in the form of welfare payments called Earned Income Credits, which are exactly the opposite as the more you make the less percentage gets return to you. Notice rich people paid for World War I and II, but after the war the very rich were overburdened with taxes so many ways to hide money was used and much of the money that could have stayed in the United States left for all parts of the world.

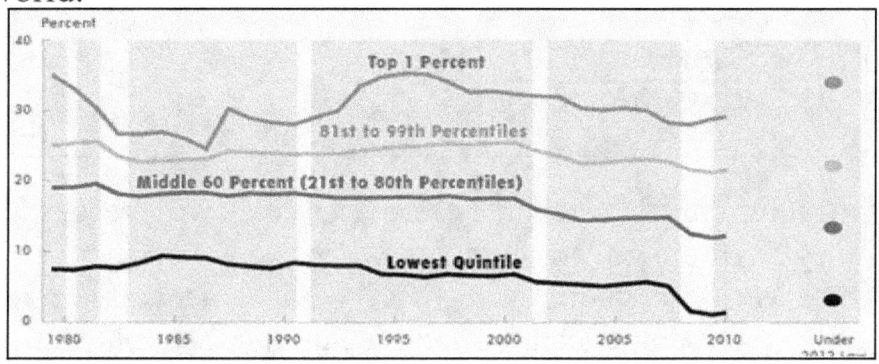

The chart above shows that the lowest 80% paying less and less since 1980 in addition to something else. Today the taxing is somewhat less stupid, but still the rich pay still pay twice the percentage as the middleclass and the low income people now make money instead of paying anything with Earned Income.

Earned Income-Notice in the graph to the let below that for someone with 3 kids, they could make $6000 instead of paying income tax. It is getting so bad that **today ½ the people pay nothing** and most get money from the government for not making enough money. If they work, the money is taken away/ the chart below right shows this negative tax bracket completely punished if they work.

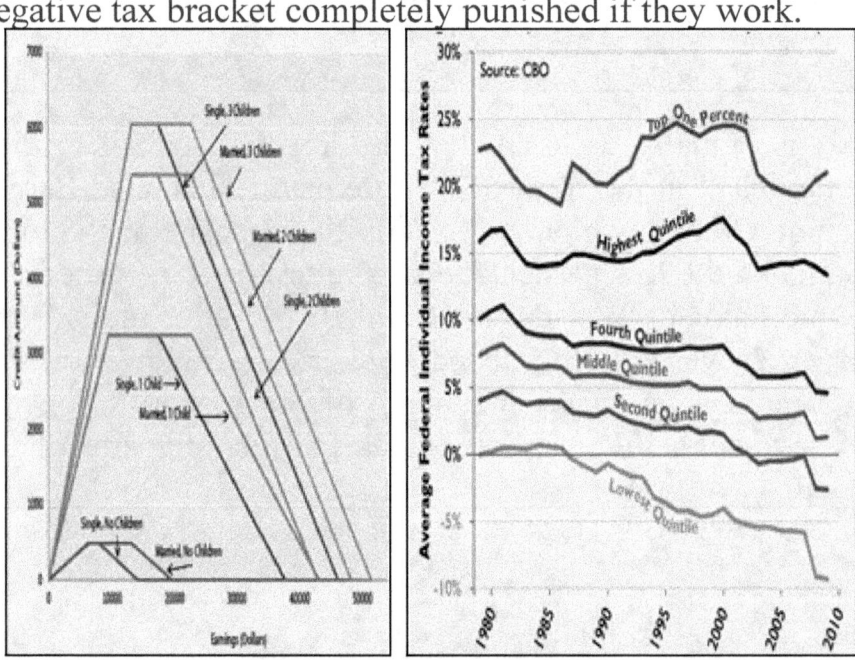

How long can this go on before everyone will be getting money from the government and when the government says bark everyone is required to bark. What is needed is more training so people can get jobs, but our schools are in horrible shape.

Fix Our Schools

One way to determine if there is a problem in our schools is to compare the standings of our schools. What we find is that many areas of our schools systems are failing in every way. The first chart shows the United State education rating from those that graduated high school and college 40 years ago as compared with how well our schools were doing 10 years ago. The chart shows that the United States is falling fast as our children are losing out by a failed system when compared to the rest of the world.

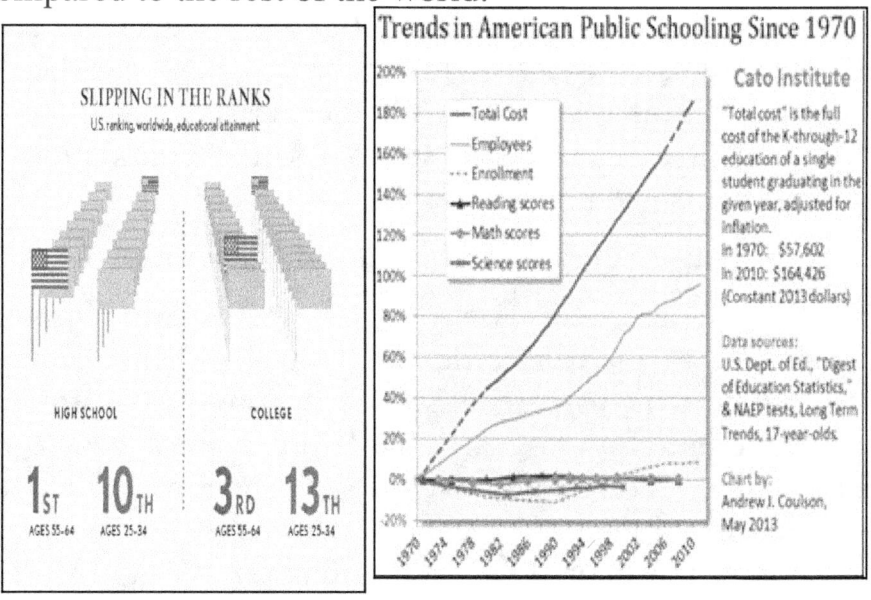

Rising Cost of Education

This phenomenon is certainly not because we are not spending enough money on them. Look at the horrible results of the second chart. Over the last 80 years with almost no difference in enrolment, reading and math scores have remained the same and science scores have fallen while we have twice as many teachers and spending almost 4 times as much for each student to experience the horror. If you are worried, you should be. You could just blame the teachers and say twice as many teachers should be making our schools better, but that is not the problem. The problem is WHAT WE ARE TEACHING. The schools today are not teaching Math, Science, History, Americanism, and honor. They are twisting everything and teaching whatever is most comfortable, whatever assures a student will pass a class, whatever will SEEMINGLY show ethnic and religious tolerance when they are actually pushing Intolerance, Hatred, Bullying, and Segregation of all students. No one can learn in that atmosphere. Hopefully, we can get to the bottom of a number of the issues. To start off, let's look at order. Without order, there can be no learning. One of the reasons for the massive reduction in order and discipline in our schools is the elimination of corporal punishment.

Praise Scholastics Instead of Disruption

While there are still some States that allow corporal punishment to increase order and focus in schools, very little can be done as parents sue the schools for "harming" their children. How bogus!!! If we don't get a handle on establishing order in our classrooms, soon we will need high fences around the schools and have to check for weapons at the door. Oh, wait a minute! We already are doing that. Getting swatted on the behind for disrupting a classroom reduces disruption. Simply asking a disrupter to keep it down only encourages the action. This extends beyond the classroom to bullying, fighting, and all type of disorder. It is a wonder that students can get any scholastic updates in our schools today. Just imagine if a child was publicly swatted for cursing and throwing spit wads and hitting classmates and all the other things that are common today. There might be fewer incidences and more order in the classrooms so our children could learn there what they need for school and what they need beyond school when working with others. In the hallways, there may be fewer fights. Students would quit ignoring the instructors and grades would increase. Outside the classroom there might be fewer road rage issues, workplace blow ups, etc. as America begins to rebuild its once great place in the world.

If a child needs to be dropped out because he is simply too hostile, then DROP HIM OUT. Don't punish the others for what he does, don't halt training our future scientists to take care of insolence, and don't fill him with drugs either.

Medicating Brains-Attention deficit hyperactivity disorder (ADHD), is the new catch phrase to keep children from squirming or learning. Without corporal punishment and with our school pride, and without praise for scholastic achievements, our students fidget, look out windows and talk to friends. Their disruption in classes are quickly fixed with drugs that turn the students into zombies all the while many are trying to convince us that the children are doing better. Unfortunately, the drugs were in some ways worse that this ADHD. My grandson was on the number one "stimulant treatments [Ritalin] for a while. He begged his mom to allow him to function without the stuff and she finally gave in. He did so much better without that stuff that it was not even funny, but today, versions of that horrible drug are still being used and destroying potentials for children to learn simply because they were disruptive and no one was allowed to use corporal punishments without

43

fear of being sued. Drugs calm them down sometimes, but in every testable way, they destroyed the kids. The next chart shows that there are SERIOUS side effects with 90% of the PATIENTS. Including increased irritability and depression which are the things it supposedly treated.

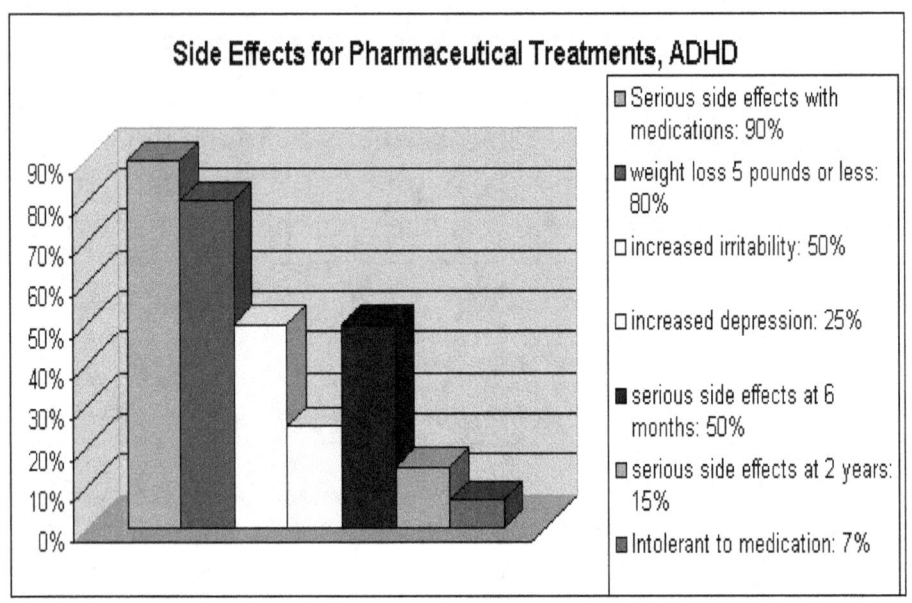

Besides affecting learning, the drugs increase medical issues, but at least the school doesn't have to spank kids. In fact, the government figured out that if they get more involved everything will be great and "No Child Left Behind" was created. What a fiasco!!!

No Child Left Behind Disaster

No Child Left Behind was enacted in 2001 and it has sped up the process of the destruction of our schools. Instead of eliminating this horror, President Obama issued an enhanced version of this stupidity in 2015 called Every Student Succeeds Act (ESSA). One thing is for certain trying to make the lowest of the low student the "success" level will only spell disaster.

Instead of removing disruptive students, someone came up with the LAW: NO CHILD LEFT BEHIND. What it really means is EVERYONE IS LEFT BEHIND the rest of the world.

This has got to stop. This stupid project was defined as 5 goals and all have been failures.

Performance Goal 1 &2: All students will reach proficiency in language arts and mathematics. As shown below left, every year we get farther and farther behind the goals of the law. By 2011 48% of the schools in America failed this first level.

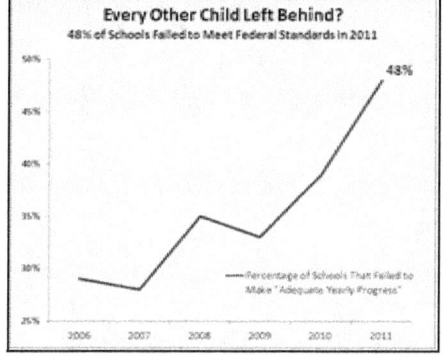

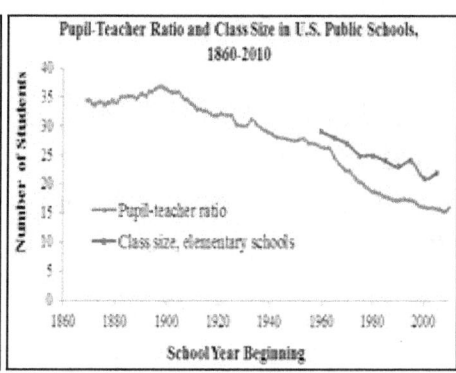

All the while, the government is spending substantially more each year. The chart, proceeding right, shows we tried to have more teachers per student. Since 1965 the number of teachers to students has been increasing dramatically as our training level has been dropping significantly. As a different issue with our schools, the next chart from the Teacher's Union may show a slightly different problem. While the government spends more and more, the money doesn't go to the classroom and the public school system gets more and more corrupt and inefficient leaving less money for teachers rather than more as always happens when State controls are converted to Federal controls. The problems are somewhere in between.

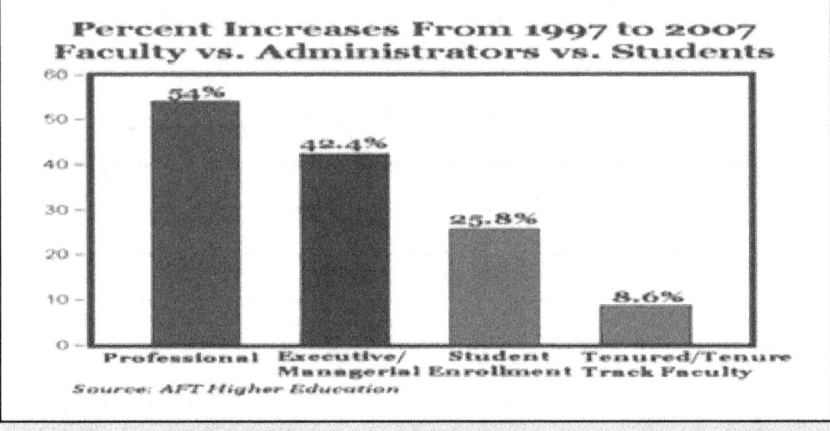

Performance Goal 3: All students will be taught by highly qualified teachers. [*The chart below left shows the disparity of white and Asian reading compared with Black and Hispanic reading scores. The 2 upper levels are white/Asian. Please notice how much closer the lines are after the law-----zero!*]

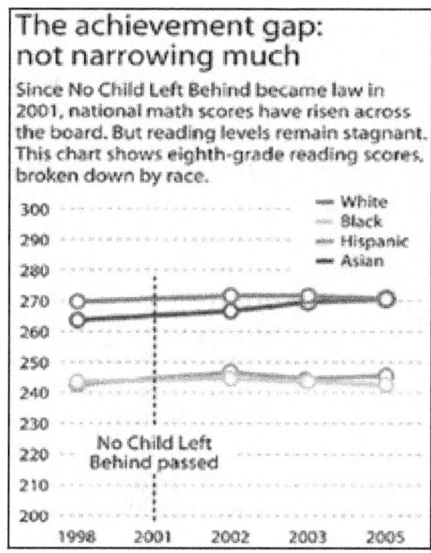

The achievement gap: not narrowing much

Since No Child Left Behind became law in 2001, national math scores have risen across the board. But reading levels remain stagnant. This chart shows eighth-grade reading scores, broken down by race.

— White
— Black
— Hispanic
— Asian

No Child Left Behind passed

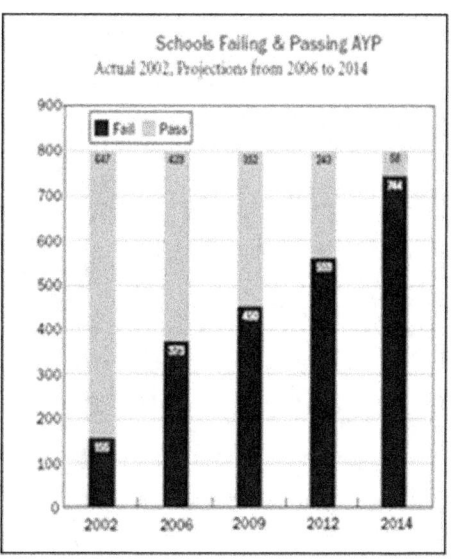

Schools Failing & Passing AYP
Actual 2002, Projections from 2006 to 2014

Fail   Pass

Performance Goal 4: All students will be educated in learning environments that are safe, drug-free, and conducive to learning. *[Reality is that 14 percent of eighth graders, 28 percent of 10th graders, and 36 percent of 12th graders used an illicit substance during the past year.]*

Performance Goal 5: All students will graduate from high school. *[While it is well known that many are being pushed out of High School without an education, the chart below is another showing the number of schools failing what is called "Acceptable Yearly Progress" AYP is getting worse and worse and worse.]* [See graph preceding right]

Suicides-By the way; the number of suicides, teen assaults, depression, and undisciplined students has skyrocketed since the leniency of the schools, reduction of corporal punishment, and this "no child left behind". Speaking of undisciplined and unlearned, let's look at a recent college survey.

College Survey-Recent surveys in colleges asked very difficult questions including:

- *Who is our Vice President?*
- *When was our Revolutionary War and who did we fight?*
- *What was the Civil War fought about and who won?*
- *Who lost the Battle of Little Bighorn?*
- *Cleopatra, was the monarch of what country?*
- *What is the highest mountain range in South America?*
- *What show is Snooky on?*

And many similar questions ----Almost NONE of the college kids knew ANY of the answers. I mean they only knew the last one. No child was finally starting to show results. The next chart shows the remarkable progress of our government push to insure the dumbest student did not feel bad and that the smartest children were simply ignored.

Eliminating Free Thinking

Another thing we need to fix besides complete disruption of what schools were meant to do [teach], we find an alarming trend to turn children into non-thinkers. One of the ways this is done is by carefully building questions to mold their minds into becoming more dependent on the federal government. Let me give you an example. The classwork below was simply entitled *Are You A Democrat Or A Republican.* It sounds innocuous enough, but read the descriptions.

Are-you-a-Democrat-or-Republican?		
Read the following issues and beliefs then select the party that shares the same belief as you.		
Issue	**Party Belief**	**D or R**
Abortion	D – It is a woman's right and should be legal. R – It should be illegal and restricted by the government	
Gun Control	D – control is necessary and the government says who can or cannot own one R – should not be controlled but responsible people can purchase if they choose	
Health-care	D – Everyone should be able to have health care regardless of income R – If you cannot pay then you will make a lot of payments or not have any care	
Taxes	D – Make the wealthy people pay more than the poor or less fortunate R – Cutting taxes for all people helps our economy and saves money for later on	
Military	D – Spend less on sending troops away for war and give more to veterans that fought R – Spend more for sending troops and don't give veterans any more than we have to	
Death Penalty	D – Against it – does not prevent crime and criminals should go to treatment centers R – For it – It should be considered only in certain situations and could prevent more	
Prayer in Schools	D – You should not pray in school because not everyone has the same beliefs as you R – You should be able to pray in school regardless of your spiritual beliefs	
Gay Marriage	D – You should be able to marry whomever you want to R – You should only be able to marry someone of the opposite sex	
Pollution	D – Companies that heavily pollute should have to pay for their own clean-up program R – Charging companies that heavily pollute more is an extra burden to them	
Flag Burning	D – You should be able to burn the flag if you want to R – It is disrespectful to those who died in war for us and should be outlawed	
Totals:	Number checks for Democrat _____ Number of checks for Republican _____	

This was an assignment of a sixth grade student at the Milam Elementary School in Tupelo, Mississippi. Her parents were shocked when their daughter brought home this worksheet the children were to fill out. Notice the retarded questioning that forces kids to say to themselves they must be democrat or they are just mean. The abortion one doesn't even talk about the dead babies at all; the health care question say a republican would not allow health care; the Military question says republicans hate veterans; the one on gay marriage adds complete confusion; the pollution one simply says republicans pollute. Guess what is being taught in that school? This is not an isolated case.

A Colorado school gave an extremely leading political quiz to seventh graders that asked them to describe their views on a host of issues—from abortion to healthcare—and implied harshly that the liberal positions were kind and conservatives were mean. Here is one telling statement. *Liberals believe that all Americans are entitled to health care when they need it and Conservatives do not believe that Americans are entitled to health care. Should you be a liberal or Conservative?*

Scientists are Being Lost- Besides the turning children into zombies, we find that since the inception of this "No Child

Left Behind" program, agricultural jobs have been blasting downwards and replaced by people in the services industry. We are becoming a country of maids and waitresses? While industrial jobs are staying about the same or increasing at a rate much less than the GDP, service positions are being filled at a skyrocketing rate. [See next left] I suppose we are trying to get a large group to try out for Donald Duck at Disney World and destroying our country at the same time.

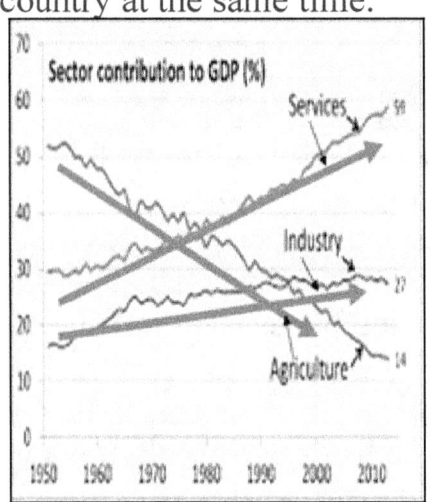
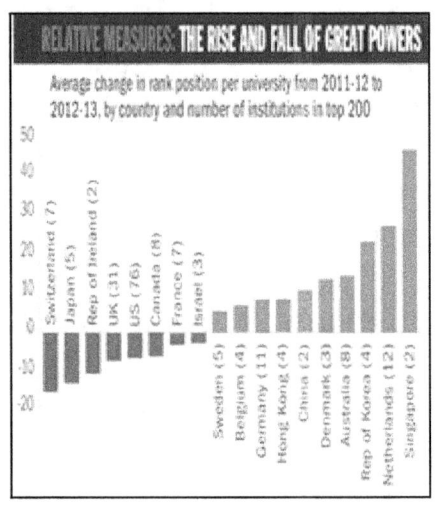

Erosion of position- As I mentioned before, the United Staee once held a position of being somewhere between 1st and 3rd in the world with respect to education, but look where we are today. The preceding right diagram shows that while many nations improve their standing, the United States is quickly eroding. In one year 2012 to 2013 we lowered our standing by 8 points. The standing from 2012 is shown below as 36th in the developed nations of the world that consists of about 36 nations.

GLOBAL EDUCATION LEAGUE TABLE				
Overall Rank*	Country/Economy	Mathematics Score	Reading Score	Science Score
1st	Shanghai (China)	613	570	580
2nd	Singapore	573	542	551
3rd	Hong Kong	561	545	555
4th	Taiwan	560	523	523
5th	South Korea	554	536	538
12th	Finland	519	524	545
26th	United Kingdom	494	499	514
36th	United States	481	498	497

Let me make this more clear so you understand just how serious this is. In 2012 test scores for what used to be the basic requirements for education Math, Reading and Science have all shown huge drops from the United States. [See above right]. The United States came in dead last on Mathematices in the bottom 25% in Reading and Science. No; they didn't provide scores for football, sex class, how to be a Muslim, why democrats are good, or dance as we would have done better. While you will not believe this, some of the athletes that are barely understanding mathematics are more well- known, more regarded, and more praised by the schools than those making phenomenal advances in understanding of some huge scientific intricacy. The vast majority of the U.S. school and educational culture is not as academically focused as the competing Asian [or any other] cultures. The Asian tiger culture highly revolves around pushing their children to do better and better in school with strong reinforcement from their parents, teachers, and their entire social and peer group. Education is emphasized heavily in these countries because it means a country can survive. In some of the highest achieving countries, ranking in the top 3 of their class means they actually have an opportunity to go to college, which could lead them to securing a job that can support a family. Therefore; competition is fierce and their academic curriculum is rigorous, so they have to work really hard just to pass. This is not the school system that made us great.

Let's compare. The U.S. educational culture is more focused on doing well in sports or being popular. If you disrupt a class, the classmates cheer. If a student is absent too many times, there is no punishment and those receiving high honors are not praised by their fellow students as it doesn't fit the free lifestyle mold. In many cases, these priorities lead kids to being rebellious or defiant, and sometimes not doing well in school, just so they're not perceived as a nerd. The parental reinforcement is also lacking because a significant amount of households today are dual working parents, or single working moms. Whatever time and energy they may have remaining after work tends to be focused more on feeding their children then actively helping them with their studies.

Spending is not the answer- The U.S. is currently one of the top spenders of all developed nations with around $115,000 per student. Yet, countries like Hungary, Poland and Slovak Republic received a similar PISA score to us, but spend less than half the amount the U.S. does. Top performer New Zealand spends less than $30,000 per student. Another thing that is not the answer is sex. As sexual deviation and punishment for normal sexuality gets higher and higher, our society gets more debased, and closer to destruction. We had better see what is going on.

Expansion of Deviant Sex

If we want to understand why our country is failing we need to talk about moral decay. At one time we had a society based on the moral character of the Christian religion, but now all stops are loosed in a mad dash to decadence. There can be no good that will come of this. If we don't turn it around soon, the focus of life will have shifted so far towards "anything goes sex" that our country will be doomed just like the Roman Empire with their high levels of debauchery just before the final end of a once great kingdom. OK they had other problems too but let's look at sexual decadence and how we are teaching our children that "anything goes sexual experimentation" should be the focus of their lives.

Condoms in Sixth Grade- Our schools have figured out how to expand sex in our children. The answer is to start before high school teaching them there should be no limits to sex. If there is a desire, they should act on those desires. Now they are handing out condoms to Middle School students without any notification to parents for children who want to experiment with sex outside of marriage. What could go wrong for the California children?

Pornographic Studies- High Schoolers get a special treat. While Reading, Writing, and Arithmetic suffer in our current schools, one area abounded to do even more harm.

Called sex education, this is tearing our scholastic component of schools to pieces as kids are being forced to examine their sexuality, permissiveness, sexual identity, and even their biologic sex as opposed to what they think they should be. Since before 1990, pornographic images like that shown below. Demonstrate methods for heterosexual encounters as well and homosexual deviations. The Minnesota High School instructor below demonstrates anal intrusion for the children.

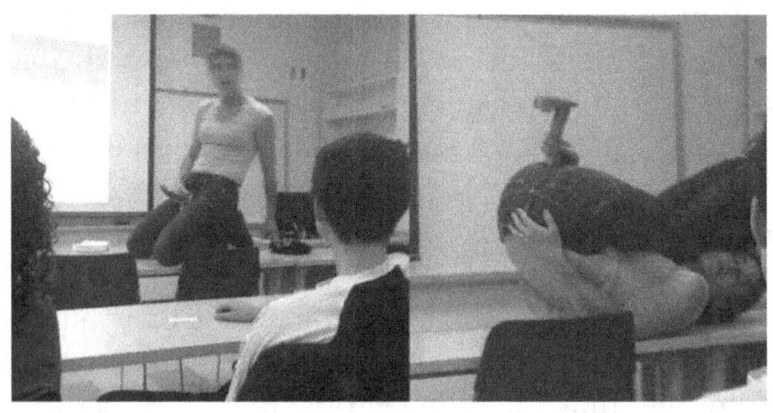

This pornographic education is keeping students minds active. The problem is that they are not being activated to do scholarly things. 2011 Centers for Disease Control and Prevention (CDC) survey indicates that more than 47 percent of all high school students say they have had sex; and 15 percent of high school students have had sex with four or more partners. The United States has the highest teen birth rate in the industrialized world. Three in 10 girls in will be pregnant at least once before their 20th birthday. Teenage mothers are less likely to finish high school. About 3.2 million adolescent females have been infected with the STI called Human papillomavirus [HPV] which is about 35 percent of teens ages 14 to 19. Girls age 15 to 19 have the highest rates of Gonorrhea. Approximately 24 percent of new HIV diagnoses were young people age 13 to 24. One study of 9th grader sexual intercourse is shown below.

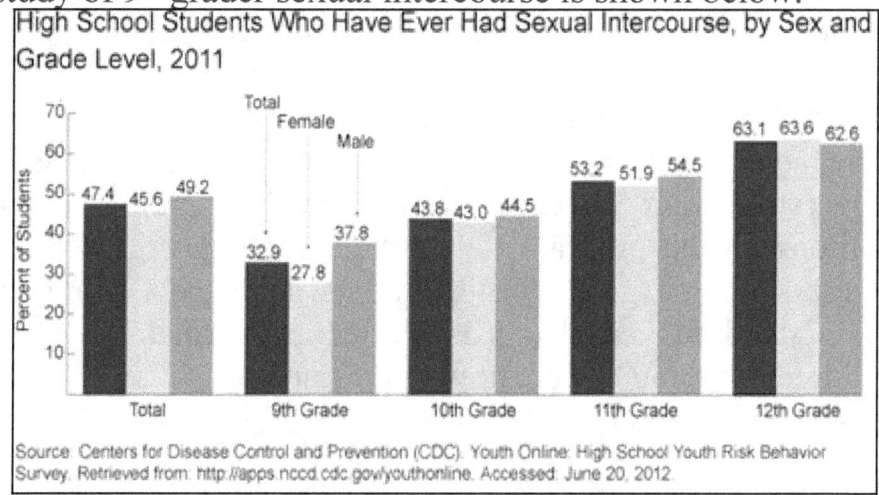

High School Students Who Have Ever Had Sexual Intercourse, by Sex and Grade Level, 2011

Source: Centers for Disease Control and Prevention (CDC). Youth Online: High School Youth Risk Behavior Survey. Retrieved from: http://apps.nccd.cdc.gov/youthonline. Accessed: June 20, 2012.

When just looking at sexual activity, the numbers get worse. The following shows the trend of sexual activity of little 9th graders being subjected to Sex classes. With fewer classes, in 1991, we see the percentage of children is about 76%. By 2011, the instruction has allowed the activity <u>to increase</u> to 78%. I'm so glad they are teaching this instead of History. The second graph may even be more telling.

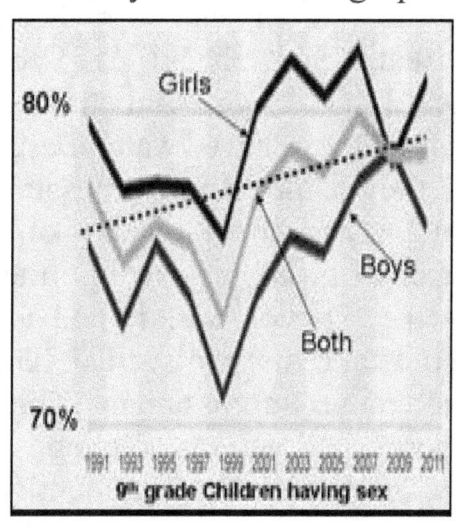

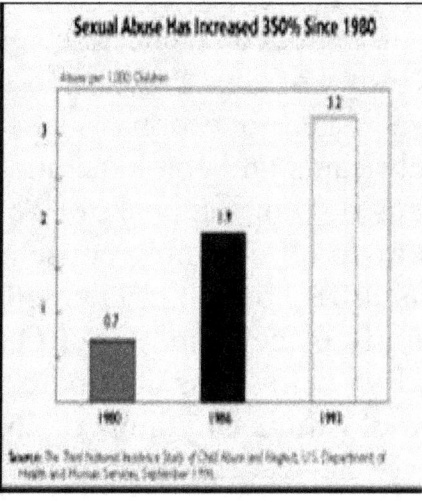

Since 1980 sexual abuse has <u>increased by 350%.</u> These abusers learned in our high schools. During the same session as depicted previously, little girls were being given detailed instructions how to strip and how to strap on artificial penises under a federally MANDATED <u>Common Core educational standard</u>. While some may think this is perversion, our government is spending hundreds of millions on the program rather than teaching high school. One book being given to 4th graders under new Common Core standards entitled "It's Perfectly Normal", <u>teaches children as young as nine how to masturbate."</u>

MeteroSexual Teachings

If all this wasn't enough to expand the debasement of the sexual character of the United States, ninth grade students at a California high school, and other locations, are learning more than just the birds and the bees as part of this Common Core destruction. Today we hear about something they call Metro-sexuality rather than hetero-sexuality. I know they sound the same, but they are soooo very different. Included in the materials provided to students about this metro sexuality were documents and worksheets that included a checklist entitled, "Sex Check! Are You Ready For Sex?" in which the 13 and 14-year-old students are asked questions such as if they have water–based lubricants and condoms and if they could handle a possible infection or pregnancy. Another worksheet reads like a how-to on obtaining consent from a possible sexual partner and offers possible statements like "Do you want to go back to my place?" and "Is it OK if I take my pants off?". The poster below was distributed so that no impressionable child would think anything of inappropriate actions, feeling, or desires. It describes a sliding scale for Gender Identity, Gender Expressiveness, Biological sex [which is downplayed substantially], and Sexual orientation. The poster touts an innocent looking bi-sexual genderbread man pictured next.

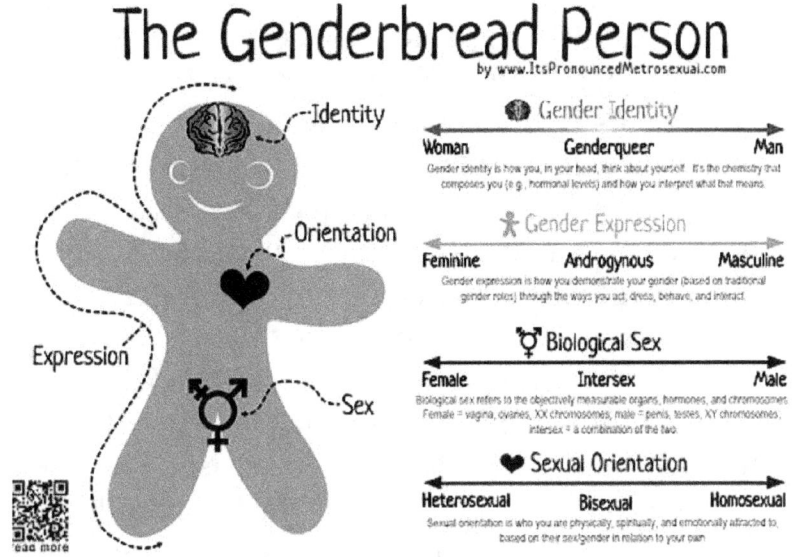

The Genderbread Person
by www.ItsPronouncedMetrosexual.com

Now our students can increase their thought about sex, and sexual attitudes from the normal 75% to almost all the time so that no learning can be accomplished. As we slip farther away from having a society for the general population welfare.

What Can we Do?

While many will not want to do these things, they are all required if we are to get out of this mess.

1. Stop making Sex alright!!!!!

2. Stop keeping sexual conduct of children away from parents.

3. Put sex education back in the home and quit confusing students with bogus claims that they should not be male or female.

Another thing is to halt the acceptance and even praise of deviant lifestyles over normalcy.

Quit Ignoring Pedophilia

Even our schools seem to focus on quieting issues concerning pedophilia in gay societies and instead bully the non-gay students so that there is less pride in scholastics, more hatred for the oddballs, and less understanding of normalcy, and far less caution around those that could harm them greatly. With respect to quieting concerns of gayness, the schools seem to worry that people might get the "wrong idea" about homosexuals, namely that their community has a special predilection toward pedophilia. Not only are there substantially more male children that have indicated they were sexually abused in general; but also, homosexuals, particular the male variety, engage in kiddy-diddling at a rate far beyond the rest of the population. Certainly, not all child molesters are homosexual, and not all homosexuals are child molesters, but the overlapping between the two groups is too large to ignore.

*About one third of pedophilia victims are boys and **nearly one hundred percent of the offenders are gay men**.*

Anyone can do the math, but it doesn't seem to come out in our schools to protect our children and guide them away from those actions. If you didn't do the math already, that means that male homosexuals, who represent about 1.5 to 2% of the population, account for approximately 33% of pedophilia incidents.

In other words, male homosexuals molest children at a rate twenty-times greater than their share of the population.

Stop the North American Man Boy Love Association

It wasn't long ago when America's premiere pedophile rights organization, the North American Man Boy Love Association (NAMBLA), marched in "gay" pride parades; in fact they marched with them for about 15 years. According to gay journalist Benoit Denizet-Lewis, the only reason NAMBLA has been staying home since 1994 is that they got too much pressure from what we call the Religious Right. The schools had nothing to say and many others simply stayed quiet so the group that does this pedophilia at a rate **15 to 20 times more frequently** than regular people. The self-identified child rapists didn't shame the non-pedophile gays and the schools are doing the same thing at the dishonor of those not in this group.

Don't Praise the "Gay, Lesbian, Straight, Education Network"

That brings us to Harry Hay, called "the father of gay liberation," fought to have the NAMBLA considered as an important part of gay pride. What he said is very telling. *"If the parents and friends of gays are truly friends of gays, they would know from their gay kids that the relationship with an older man is precisely what thirteen-, fourteen-, and fifteen-year-old kids need more than anything else in the world."* This pedophilia stance, promoted by our schools by quiet absolution, is not being stifled at all; in fact, the Gay Lesbian Straight Education Network's (GLSEN's) recommended reading list for kids includes books that depict (and excuse) homosexual encounters between adults and children.

Multiple Studies-A study in the *"Archives of Sexual Behavior"* ... *Recent surveys estimate the prevalence of homosexuality, among men attracted to adults, in the neighborhood of 2%. In contrast, the prevalence of* *homosexuality among pedophiles may be as high as 30 - 40%."*

A study in the *"**Journal of Sex Research**"* noted that *"... the proportion of sex offenders against male children among homosexual men is <u>substantially larger</u> than the proportion of sex offenders against female children among heterosexual men-*

A study of 229 **convicted child molesters** published in another report from the *"**Archives of Sexual Behavior**"* found that *"<u>**eighty-six percent**</u> of [sexual] offenders against males described themselves as homosexual or bisexual."*

Still another study from the *Archives of Sexual Behavior* found that "The rate of homosexual attraction is <u>6-20 times higher among pedophiles.</u>"

The *"**Institute for Sex Research**"*, which was founded by Alfred Kinsey, determined *that 25% of white homosexual men have had sex with boys sixteen years and younger.*

An editorial in the *"**San Francisco Sentinel**"*, [from a gay journalist] stated something telling. *"The love between men and boys is at the foundation of homosexuality. For the gay community to imply that boy love is not homosexual love is ridiculous. We must not be seduced into believing misinformation from the press and the government. Child molesting does occur, but <u>there are also positive sexual relations. And we need to support the men and the boys in those relationships.</u>"* **[I just vomited a little.]**

Don't Focus on One Wife

When it comes to figuring out how the Supreme Court will move in a deviant sex world, you just never know.

1890- The U.S. Supreme Court ruled that **polygamy could not be practiced** in the United States, stating that: *It is contrary to the spirit of Christianity and the civilization which Christianity has produced in the Western world.*

While there is no constitutional reason for the federal government to take away States right in this matter, they did it. They reasoned, "Some are disgusted seeing a man with 2 women and there are bad States out there that will allow it, so we will simply take their rights away."

1973-*Roe* v. *Wade-* legalized abortion in all States even if they disagreed.

1986- While killing babies was OK, **t**he Court decided two men having sex and Sodomy were against the law

1992-*Planned Parenthood v. Casey* - The court then decided the Fetus did have some rights and a Doctor must decide if killing it was justified. Judge O'Connor stated this- *At the heart of liberty is the right to define one's own concept of existence, of meaning, of the universe, and of the mystery of human life. Beliefs about these matters could not define the attributes of personhood were they formed under compulsion of the State.*

1996- *State Sanctioned Gay Marriage-*This court indicated the Defense of Marriage Act (DOMA) was unconstitutional that it violated the rights of gays and lesbians. The court also ruled that the law interferes with the states' rights to define marriage.

1996- *Deviant Same Sex in California-* The Supreme Court taking away State's rights farther ruled that same-sex marriage referendum [Proposition 8] was not legal opponents in California did not have standing to appeal the lower court ruling that overturned the state's ban, known as

Proposition 8. The ruling would most likely remove legal battles for same-sex couples wishing to marry in California. However, the ruling did not directly affect other states.

2000- Boy Scouts v. Dale, the Court ruled that the Boy Scouts' First Amendment rights of free expression and association meant gay Scoutmasters must be allowed to train our children.

2003- If Gays were going to be scout masters, the court now decided Sodomy was OK.

2006- *Forced Easier Abortions-*This court made abortions easier by not requiring a 48 hour parental notification no matter what States said.

2007- *Forced Even Easier Abortions-* This court made abortions easier by no long restricting for a mother's Health no matter what States said.

2013 - *United States v. Windsor-* This decision changed the meaning of Marriage to include boy-boy. The court ruled that the Defense of Marriage Act is unconstitutional.

2015- Forced Deviant Same sex marriage ruling-The Court ruled that same-sex couples have the fundamental right to marry in any State and that States cannot say that marriage is reserved for heterosexual couples.

Didn't like to See Things

The Supreme Court ruled that a husband can have only one wife. This was not done because of something in the Constitution; it was done because some didn't like seeing a man with 2 wives. As I mentioned, the Bible only stipulates that if a man wants to be a deacon of a church, he must restrict the number of wives to one. Currently that interpretation is still on the books as a "MORE moral than the Bible" characterization of our laws that were based on

Biblical baselines. If we are trying to establish some more godly action in America, we should first restrict the number of times one can be married sequentially divorce after divorce. While those things are not that disruptive nor do they establish a more deviant lifestyle, the Supreme Court continues with the multiple wife stupidity and initially it worked to reduce deviant sex by ruling against sodomy.

Supreme Court Against Sodomy

If you think a man with 2 women made them mad, this got the federal judges ready to take away more States rights as they feared the worst.

While there is no constitutional reason for the federal government to take away States right in this matter, they did it. They reasoned, "Some are disgusted seeing a man and a man stuck together and there are bad States out there that will allow it, so we will simply take their rights away."

Later sodomy was tested and determined to be a jail-able offence to the community not only because it was disgusting to the majority, but also that it was determined to be a deviation from the majority by any measure possible and completely detestable according to Biblical descriptions. Certainly, the court softened the punishment from the more strict Jewish law, but it was certainly described as a deviation from Constitutional value [but it was to be judged by individual States only].

Oh No!!!!!!As we move up in time we find that the decision was repealed so that men could kiss men in public etc. MANY had disgust watching 2 guys kissing each other or whatever that deviate lifestyle has as a public past time, but *the majority was rammed in a corner to push the* *deviant lifestyle as the General Welfare was stabbed.* Let me give you a similar example.

Similar Deviation-*Once there was a boy how had an urge to pass gas on his food before he ate it. It was something about the aroma that was tantalizing to him. He kept his urges a secret for some time, but some someone at school saw him and called him a fart-eater. He went to the principle and told him he had no right to say ugly things as he decided that his habit was because of his DNA was defective, in fact he found another that passed gas on his food in school and both petitioned the principle, "If people continue to call me a fart-eater, I will feel uncomfortable passing gas on my food!" Not long afterwards, there was a sign indicating that it was un-American to call people by names they didn't like and that flatulent-smeller was the only name allowed for the unusual teens. This continued. Not long after this incident one of the flatulent-smellers was in a restaurant and flavored his food as he normally did and the restaurant owner made him leave. The federal government fined the restaurant even though he explained he would lose customers as no one could eat after witnessing the habit. The fed didn't care and told the man that if he could not provide the constitutional right for the flatulent-smeller he would not be allowed to own a restaurant as the action was protected by the Constitution. [Even though it was not] The flatulent-smellers requested that they be given special privilege like getting tax breaks for being joined as a family of flatulent-smellers even though to some, the habit was against their moral code. Soon flatulent-smellers were allowed to adopt children so they could teach them how to flatulent-smell. A national "adult flatulent-smelling with children" foundation was established and it was found out that a much higher* *percentage of flatulent-smellers had their adopted children flatulent-smell against their will than normal people and still adoptions were allowed. Soon all were required to flatulent-smell when going to a restaurant. If they did not flatulent-smell they would have to be removed. Even as the flatulent-smeller indicated his "condition" was genetic, identical twins did not both show this disgusting trait, but he kept saying it anyway. Soon the government outlawed open prayer but required people to watch flatulent-smelling.*

I know this sounds like *flatulent-smellers* should not be kept from doing whatever they wanted to do so long as the Constitution didn't say it was bad, but let's think about it for a second as deviants are deviant for a reason, they go against common levels of decency and bending to those ways will soon disrupt the moral fiber of a country. The same thing can be said about the following:

- **Snake licking**-even if a small group had urges to do this; it would not help the moral character of our nation.

- **Not wearing clothes in public**- even is a small group had urges to disrobe; it would not help moral character of those witnessing the group action.

- **A man marrying a man**- even if a small group had urges to do this, it would not help the moral character of our nation, especially given the huge implications of sexual misconduct that has been observed in such a climate.

- **Making pornographic movies**- While not a constitutional matter and some see no issue, there is no reason not to have laws against these things even though there is no Constitutional issue at all.

- **A male man marrying a female animal**- Again, some may think their DNA is forcing it, but it can be disruptive to society. Sure it is more reasonable than 2 men having sex, but it is still a deviant lifestyle.

- **Baby-killing to reduce a need for Planned Parenthood**- Certainly there can be something to be said for eliminating children who would put pressure on a country's resources, but here we are looking a "moral stuff". Morally, killing sounds bad just like or possibly worse that two men kissing.

Sorry I got carried away. Let me continue by looking at Transvestites. My opinion is I don't care how people dress or what they think of their own body, but I don't want it flaunted or described as being acceptable for children to confuse them and force us away from welfare for the general public and concentration on the deviations.

No more Coddling Transvestism

I'm all for insuring that all our kids have opportunity to learn in a safe environment, but what is happening with this absurdity is that we are eliminating protection by coddling the abnormal. Certainly, we must guard against hoodlum threats, attacks, and bigotry to reasonable levels but not to the extent of shaming normalcy and reducing the basic protections our children need to be in a comfortable atmosphere for learning. Not only is there a real safety issue, but also there are ramifications as normal no longer becomes desirable. This is a slippery slope that cannot be easily turned.

Transvestitism Orders- I know the new term is Transgenderism, but now in our schools, anyone wearing female clothes **must** go to the women's dressing rooms. Yeah right!!!!! Another command in the new order is that all men that think they are women on the inside can and should try out for women's sports. Unbelievably, the deviate men in dresses win the competitions. Soon, the transvestites or transsexuals or whatever cause massive reductions the moral fabric of the school, increase sexual misconduct, and destroy any opportunity of a real girl to compete normally. While there should be tolerance, we cannot disregard the fact that this is a deviation from normalcy to not be praised, highlighted, or put on a pedestal of greatness.

Minnesota High School League-A new policy from the Minnesota High School League [MHSL] concerning Transgenderism says *if a boy says he is a girl, he must be allowed to use girl bathroom, play on girl teams and act like a girl.* There is sort of an exemption of religious schools it goes like this. *"If a private religious school claims their exemption they lose some standing in the league? Will they be forced to forfeit certain games? Will they be forced to allow visiting schools on their facilities to allow their students to use facilities of the opposite sex?*

Federal Office of Civil Rights, Title IX-Writing on behalf of the NFHS, one of the Massachusetts leaders advises every high school administrator in America that, *"The Federal Office of Civil Rights, Title IX requires that boys pretending to be girls, and girls pretending to be boys, must be permitted to compete on, and share locker room and showering facilities with, the sports teams of the opposite sex."* [I paraphrased] She further objects, *"Practices such as requiring them to use locker rooms and bathrooms that correspond to their gender <u>assigned at birth</u> discourages participation. The belief that transgender girls are not 'real' girls is sometimes expressed as a concern,"*

67

There is no question that these abnormal individuals should be discouraged from participation. Additionally, you are not "assigned a gender". You have a gender and you can be normal or not.

Identical twin studies have shown one gay or transsexual with the other [with exactly the same DNA] is normal. The classrooms are not a place to experiment with these things. It should be a place of study.

Many people believe pubescent boys have more testosterone than girls and would be bigger, stronger, and faster, making sports twisted in favor of the Transgender girls but that is just a myth unless transgender girls ARE NOT real girls. Pumping kids full of dangerous hormones or mutilating their genitalia changes none of this and identifying transgenderism as being normal helps tear down the delicate fabric that allows our children to learn in our schools. This forced pride in abnormalcy is very dangerous when it comes to pedophilia, and transgender attitudes, and deviant sexual attitudes as they force the lowest form of man's debased nature. We must try to uplift rather than wallow or soon only wallowing in the sexual mire. It's like a drug addict. The more he wallows, the worse he will become. The best possible way to return to useful life is to stop taking drugs.

Halt the Rise of Sex by Our Youth

The sad report following shows that black people by far are not only participating in more sex, but also transmitting disease at a great number. This in no way is to suggest black people are the only ones suffering from the attempts to make sex glamorous and anything goes attitudes are not only acceptable but expected.

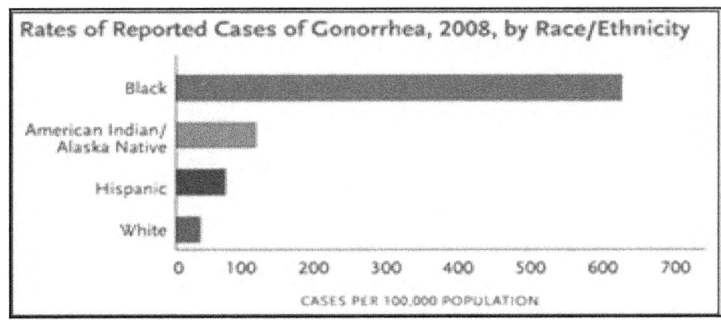

Rates of Reported Cases of Gonorrhea, 2008, by Race/Ethnicity

CASES PER 100,000 POPULATION

We have a serious problem that is now affecting our entire country as sexual "free spirit" no matter what attitudes are encroaching on the population social and business attitude cause lacadazical work ethic, limited pride in the work environment, and focus away from building our country.

Re-read the First Amendment

Madison's original proposal for a bill of rights provision concerning religion read: *"The civil rights of none shall be abridged on account of religious belief or worship, nor shall any national religion be established, nor shall the full and equal rights of conscience be in any manner, or on any pretense, infringed."* The language was altered in the House to read: "Congress shall make no law establishing religion, or to prevent the free exercise thereof, or to infringe the rights of conscience. Finally it was adopted as: *Congress shall make no law respecting an establishment of religion, or prohibiting the free exercise thereof; or abridging the freedom of speech, or of the press, or the right of the people peaceably to assemble, and to petition the Government for a redress of grievances.*

Wow! What a change! It is not known if the House readdressed this petition with all these changes, but notice "Congress shall make no law that infringes of provided the pretense on the rights of conscience" was removed.

The question is what in the world does this mean? As almost all of the people in the United States at the time, it represented not allowing one **"Christian Religion"** over another as was seen in France, England, Ireland, Germany and just about everywhere in Europe to take focus away from our creator God who could help guide our country into prosperity. Certainly if the majority had been moon worshippers, various sects of Muslimism would be pushed to support religious freedom I suppose, but we have seen what that will do as prosperity in Muslim nations comes by 2 methods killing your enemy and taking their money or taking over oil fields.

Resume Religious Freedom

No matter what some have told you, the United States of America was founded on the God described in the Bible. Anyone who does not admit that is deliberately ignoring the preponderance of written materials and artifacts from the 100 years that encapsulate that period of American history. While it is true that exceptions existed (*Thomas Jefferson for example left behind quotes that were all over the map on this topic, and Thomas Paine was almost as bad as both were not Christian*), the weight of the evidence makes that fact clear to any truly objective student of history. While many point to articles that describe some of the Founding Fathers as Deist, they are also forced to admit that most were various Christians. None were humanist, Atheist, Snake worshiping, Muslim, or Wicca. The period of American history just preceding the American Revolution was defined principally by the "Great Awakening". This evangelistic movement occurred in the 1730's and 40's, just prior to the Revolution. During this time we find "Fire and brimstone" types of preachers, such as George Whitefield, Jonathan Edwards, Increase Mather, and John Witherspoon (*a signer of the Declaration of Independence*). These men helped shape the religious attitudes and perspectives of the colonists, the founders, and the Constitution. Besides the three Roman Catholics included with the Founding Fathers, the Protestant Convention delegates included 28

Episcopalians, 8 Presbyterians, 7 Congregationalists, 2 Lutherans, 2 Dutch reformed and 2 Methodists. As this group designed the Constitution, it would be based on Biblical principles we seem to shy away from today.

1. *Man is innately evil and must seek God to establish empathy towards his fellow men.*
2. *One must not have other Gods besides the true creator.*
3. *Be slow to anger and fast in forgiveness.*
4. *You must work for you food.*
5. *Do not kill and love your enemies*
6. *Marriage is a sacred rite between a man and woman.*
7. *Eliminate the lusts of the flesh [sexual deviation, gluttony, sloth, envy, hatred, and so on if you wish for happiness.]*
8. *Honor you family and your responsibility to them.*
9. *Do not allow the barbaric institution of Sharia Law to disrupt this nation [Oops! I added that one by mistake.]*

Yes, there are 612 laws given to the Jewish people, but this is not what I'm talking about hear as most of those were laws separate the Jewish bloodline so don't go there. Here are the words of John Hancock our fourth President who ruled at the beginning of the Revolution. He said *"We Recognize No Sovereign but God, and no King but Jesus!"* John Adams [noted as being the 2nd President after the third Constitution said this. *"The general principles upon which the Fathers achieved independence were the general principals of Christianity. I will avow that I believed and now believe that those general principles of Christianity are as eternal and immutable as the existence and attributes of God."* I know the first thing you are going to say is there is no requirement for a man to have only one wife if he is not a deacon in the Bible and there is nothing in our third Constitution about this but the Supreme Court ruled that in

America there would be no polygamy. I know some knuckle head is saying on the Island of Fiji everyone has multiple wives. We are hurting their feeling if they come to America. You are right and it was an injustice to have a ruling against polygamy, but it was for the GENERAL population welfare, not for the small group who wanted the misery of having many wives. Today we are going terribly wrong by eliminating general welfare for comfort of the minority. Many times it is the very tiniest sector of our nation that is taking away the power of majority. The first topic puts us back in school.

Forcing Muslim Cultism in Schools

In the name of the first amendment, at least one school has gotten it terribly wrong. While there are probably more, at LaPlatt High School in Maryland [public and paid by our government] forced children to memorize the Five Pillars of Islam, taught them that the faith of a Muslim is stronger than the average Christian; told them the cult as completely peaceful; told the "killing yourself to gain paradise" was a lie but described jihad war against unbelievers as a religious duty; and finally, forced them to recite the Shahada [Islamic Creed to become Muslim, "There is no god but Allah, and Muhammad is the messenger of Allah."]. While it was probably a lot worse, this tax dollar paid school spend a single day ridiculing Christianity and the catholic Pope, but spend 10 times as long forcing students to "become" Muslim cultists before one parent told the school his Christian religion would not let his daughter stay in that class any longer and they should stop it immediately, he was told she would get zeros. If we are to fix our country, the first thing should be to require all students to skip this class.

Early Courts Show Christian Religions only

While the present federal courts have "UNBELIEVABLY" identified Secular Humanism [Man is his own God] as a religion so that it now is halting all Christian moral application into our society. Before we got into this fix, there was a much less broad definition of Religion as Christian only religion. No Hindu multi-headed snake, or pear, or Witch tree, or Muslim moon, or even Deism [Belief in a single creator God without Jesus].

1584-The first colonial grant made to Sir Walter Raleigh...*and the grant authorizing him to enact statutes for the government of the proposed colony provided that they 'be not against the true Christian faith...'*

1606-The first charter of Virginia, granted by King James I...*commenced the grant in these words: '...in propagating of Christian religion to such people as yet live in darkness...'*

Language of similar import may be found in the subsequent charters of that colony...in 1609 and 1611; and the same is true of the various charters granted to the other colonies. In language more or less emphatic is the establishment of the Christian religion declared to be one of the purposes of the grant.

1620-The celebrated compact made by the Pilgrims in the Mayflower, recites: *'Having undertaken for the Glory of God, and advancement of the Christian faith...a voyage to plant the first colony in the northern parts of Virginia...'*

1638-The Fundamental Orders of Connecticut, under which a provisional government was instituted, *commence with this declaration: 'And well knowing where a people are gathered together, the Word of God requires that to maintain the peace and union...there should be an orderly and decent government established according to God...to maintain and preserve the liberty and purity of the Gospel of our Lord Jesus which we now profess...of the said Gospel [which] is now practiced amongst us.'*

1701-In the Charter of Privileges granted by William Penn to the province of Pennsylvania, it is recited: *'...No people can be truly happy, though under the greatest enjoyment of civil liberties, if abridged of...their religious profession and worship...'*

1776-Coming nearer to the present time, the Declaration of Independence recognizes the presence of the Divine in human affairs in these words: *'We hold these truths to be self-evident, that all men are created equal, that they are endowed by their Creator with certain unalienable rights...appealing to the Supreme Judge of the world for the rectitude of our intentions...And for the support of this Declaration, with firm reliance on the Protection of Divine Providence, we mutually pledge to each other our lives, our fortunes, and our sacred honor.'*

We find everywhere a clear recognition of the same truth...because of a general recognition of this truth [that we are a Christian nation]; the question has seldom been presented to the courts...

There is no dissonance in these declarations. There is a universal language pervading them all, having one meaning; they affirm and reaffirm that this is a religious nation. These are not individual sayings, declarations of private persons: they are organic utterances; they speak the voice of the entire people.

1811 [NY Supreme Court]-*The morality of the country is deeply engrafted upon Christianity, and not upon the* *doctrines or worship of other religions. In people whose manners are refined, and whose morals have been elevated and inspired with a more enlarged benevolence, it is by means of the Christian religion. Offenses against religion and morality strikes at the root of moral obligation, and weaken the security of the social ties.....This First Amendment declaration never meant to withdraw religion and with it the sanctions of moral and social obligation from all consideration and notice of the law. Whatever strikes at the root of Christianity tends manifestly to the dissolution of civil government, because it tends to corrupt the morals of the people, and to destroy good order.*

1815 [Pennsylvania Supreme Court]-*The destruction of morality renders the power of the government invalid.*

1824 [Pennsylvania Supreme Court]- *A malicious intention, to vilify the Christian religion and the scriptures, would prove a nursery of vice, a school of preparation to qualify young men for the gallows, and young women for the brothel, and there is not a skeptic of decent manners and good morals, who would not consider such a common nuisance and disgrace. No free government now exists in the world, unless where Christianity is acknowledged, and is the religion of the country. Christianity is part of the common law. Its foundations are broad and strong and deep. It is the purest system of morality and only stable support of all human laws.*

1824--While because of a general recognition of this truth the question has seldom been presented to the courts, yet we find that in -Updegraph v. the Commonwealth, it was decided that, *Christianity, general Christianity, is, and always has been, a part of the common law...not*

Christianity with an established church...but Christianity with liberty of conscience to all men.

*1844-*And in the famous case of Vidal v. Girard's Executors, this court observed: *'It is also said, and truly, that the Christian religion is a part of the common law...'If we pass beyond these matters to a view of American life as expressed by its laws, its business, its customs and its society, we find everywhere a clear recognition of the same truth. Among other matters note the following: The form of oath universally prevailing, concluding with an appeal to the Almighty; the custom of opening sessions of all deliberative bodies and most conventions with prayer; the prefatory words of all will, 'In the name of God, amen', the laws respecting the observance of the Sabbath, with the general cessation of all secular business, and the closing of courts, legislatures, and other similar public assemblies on that day; the churches and church organizations which abound in every city, town and hamlet; the multitude of charitable organizations existing everywhere under Christian auspices; the gigantic missionary associations, with general support, and aiming to establish Christian missions in every quarter of the globe. These, and many other matters which might be noticed, add a volume of unofficial declarations to the mass of organic utterances that this is a Christian nation...we find everywhere a clear recognition of the same truth. The happiness of a people and the good order and preservation of civil government essentially depend upon piety, religion and morality. Religion, morality, and knowledge are necessary to good government, the preservation of liberty, and the happiness of mankind.*

1844- [Supreme Court] - In this case, A Deist [one who believed in a creator God, but not Jesus] tried to teach his form of God in a Pennsylvanian School. Here is the ruling against Deism being in School- *Christianity...is not to be maliciously and openly reviled and blasphemed against, to the annoyance of believers or the injury of the public...It is unnecessary for us, however, to consider the establishment of a school or college, for the propagation of...Deism, or any other form of infidelity. Such a case is not to be presumed to exist in a Christian country...Why may not laymen instruct in the general principles of Christianity as well as ecclesiastics...And we cannot overlook the blessings, which such [lay] men by their conduct, as well as their instructions, may, nay must, impart to their youthful pupils. Why may not the Bible, and especially the New Testament, without note or comment, be read and taught as a divine revelation in the [school] -- its general precepts expounded, its evidences explained and its glorious principles of morality inculcated?...Where can the purest principles of morality be learned so clearly or so perfectly as from the New Testament? It is also said, and truly, that the Christian religion is a part of the common law of Pennsylvania...*

1846 [S. Carolina Supreme Court] - *Christianity has reference to the principles of right and wrong. It is the foundation of those morals and manners upon which our society is formed; it is their basis. Remove this and they would fall. Morality has grown upon the basis of Christianity. What constitutes the standard of good morals? Is it not Christianity? There certainly is none other. Say that cannot be appealed to, and what would be good morals? The day of moral virtue in which we live would, in an instant, if that standard were abolished, lapse into the dark and murky night of pagan immorality.*

1854 [House Judiciary Committee]-*Religion must be considered as the foundation on which the whole structure* *rests. In this age there can be no substitute for Christianity; the great conservative element on which we must rely for the purity and permanence of free institutions. The great vital and conservative element in our system is the belief of our people in the pure doctrines and divine truths of gospel of Jesus Christ.*

1892- **[Supreme Court]-***The happiness of a people and the good order and preservation of civil government essentially depend upon piety, religion [Christian Religion] and morality.*

1892-[Supreme Court]-*Our laws and our institutions must necessarily be based upon and embody the teachings of The Redeemer of mankind. It's impossible that it should be otherwise; and in this sense and to this extent our civilization and our institutions are emphatically Christian... This is a religious people. These, and many other matters which might be noticed, add a volume of unofficial declarations to the mass of organic utterances that this is a Christian nation.*

1948- McCollum v. Board of Education-In this powerful ruling, the Supreme Court defined the crucial and central role of Christianity in the history of American education: *Traditionally, organized education in the Western world was Church education. It could hardly be otherwise when the education of children was primarily study of the Word and the ways of God. Even in the Protestant countries, where there was a less close identification of Church and State, the basis of education was largely the Bible, and its chief purpose inculcation of piety.*

1952- Zorach v. Clauson-In this important ruling, the Supreme Court clearly defined the meaning of the First Amendment and the doctrine of "Separation of Church and

State." *The purpose of the First Amendment is merely to prohibit the establishment of an official national church, similar to England's Anglican Church.* The Founding Fathers were not trying to prohibit the federal government from supporting religious institutions, promoting a reverence for God, or even favoring Christianity over other religious faiths. According to the Supreme Court's ruling: *The First Amendment, however, does not say that in every respect there shall be a separation of Church and State. Rather, it studiously defines the manner, the specific ways, in which there shall be no concert or union or dependency one on the other. That is the common sense of the matter. Otherwise the state and religion would be aliens to each other -- hostile, suspicious, and even unfriendly.*

1982 [Joint Resolution of Congress]- *"Whereas the Bible, the Word of God, has made a unique contribution in shaping the United States as a distinctive and blessed nation of people. Whereas Biblical teachings inspired concepts of civil government that are contained in our Declaration of Independence and the Constitution of The United States ... Whereas that renewing our knowledge of, and faith in God through Holy Scriptures can strengthen us as a nation and a people. Now therefore be it resolved ... that the President is authorized and requested to designate 1983 as a national "Year of the Bible" in recognition of both the formative influence the Bible has been for our nation, and our national need to study and apply the teachings of the Holy Scriptures."*

While those show a strong affection for Christianity in our interpretation, let's back up a little and investigate these early constitutionalists and how they viewed cults outside the Christian faith as it seems that since we have been slowly moving away from a Christian mindset, our nation has been crumbling. In this case we will look at 4 major wars with the Muslims. I think a little history will show us a natural danger in moral decay.

Was Muslim Cultism to be Regarded Favorably?

From the 16th to 19th century, Muslim pirates overran thousands of ships and captured and enslaved about a million Christians from as far north as Iceland and to the west from the United States because their "religion" told them to do it. If there was no immediate use of the slaves [sex toys, or galley slaves on ships] they were forced to accept Muslim cultism and locked in large centrally located prisons for easy access. As a note about these galley slaves they were shackled to the seats where they stayed until many died; urinating, defecating, eating, and sleeping next to their oar. Americans fearing the Muslims did not address this as a religion. While the Treaty of Paris was signed in September of 1783, it wasn't until 1784 that the Americans were no longer protected by the British payments to the Muslims and the first Americans were enslaved. This continued through 2 wars [1801 and 1815] where the "Shores of Tripoli for the Marines and William Decatur's bravery were both indelibly linked to the fight against Muslim slavers.

Muslim Enslavement of Americans

In March 1786, Thomas Jefferson and John Adams went to London to negotiate with Tripoli's ambassador Sidi Haji Abdrahaman. When they enquired "concerning the ground of the pretensions to make war upon nations who had done them no injury", the ambassador told them their Religion forced it. He said: *"It was written in their Koran, that all nations which had not acknowledged the Prophet were sinners, whom it was the <u>right and duty of the faithful to</u>*

plunder and enslave; and that every Muslim who was slain in this warfare was sure to go to paradise."

In 1795, Algerian Muslims held 115 American sailors and assured return of same for a sum well over $1 million "tribute". This was very hard to come by so many of these first captives remained enslaved for over a decade. The continuing demand for tribute ultimately led to the formation of the United States Department of the Navy [in 1798] to prevent further taking of American slaves by Muslims. More enslavement followed and to hold off the Muslims they continued to pay up to $1 million per year over the next 15 years for the safe passage of American ships and the return of American slaves. To put that in perspective this was about 10 to 20% of the entire GDP back then. After our wars against Muslim aggression, most of the world had halted the expansion of slavery including the United States [1808] but it was not so for this group as they made half-baked claim of halting in 1981 and again in 2007, but even today, this practice is still common in Chad, Mauritania, Niger, Mali, Sudan and other Muslim strongholds.

Our nation knew and feared the Muslims and without question did not consider this particular cult which professed getting to heaven by killing and enslaving Christians as a religion nor did they assume snake worship, devil worship, or the belief that there was no God, or the cults associated with the rites of Mother Nature. For instance, the religion of Wicca was dealt with quickly and without mercy because of a similar fear as Americans had for the Muslims. I'm certainly not thinking killing witches is right, but you cannot force witch actions in a school or praise that religion as Christianity is stepped on. There is absolutely no question about this, but somewhere along the line the Constitution was, essentially, rewritten in a devastating way. Tolerance gave way to equal opportunity, which gave way to stifling Christianity at almost all cost. As this change of moral attitude away from the initial meaning of the Constitution took the nation, our decay was well noted as our country began to die.

Less Christian Seems to be a Problem

A Gallop Poll reports that Christian Americans are declining in number. The report shows that in the first year of tracking, 1948, 91% of Americans identified themselves as belonging to some form of Christianity. The Gallop report conducted in 2008 showed this number had declined to 77% of Americans who identify themselves as belonging to some sort of Christianity. The same Gallop poll reported that in 1948 only 2% of Americans reported no religious affiliation while in 2008, 12% of Americans claimed no religious affiliation. It appears that Americans are in fact "losing our faith." The next image left shows the relatively fast rise of humanists, but the chart to the right clearly shows this is the largest religion shift in the world. While the basic Christian ideals are crucial in securing a stable country they are not the only thing we need to look at, but just as fast as our country is falling apart, the number of Christians is abandoning Christianity.

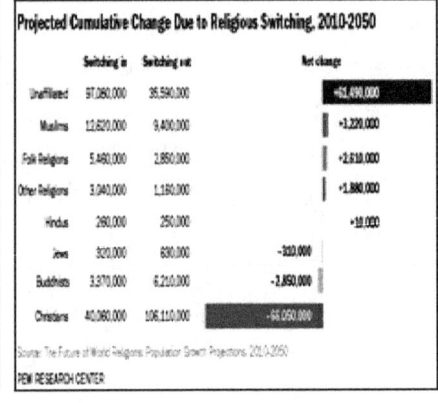

Acceptance of Cultists Seems to be a Problem

So we have a Constitution written by Christian leaders fearing the Muslim hordes taking their citizens and enslaving them such that they had a well-defined meaning for religion as any Christian religion. All of a sudden, someone turned it upside down and said we need to coddle the following:

1. Muslim, moon god cultists, whose morality is centered on getting to heaven with 72 virgins by killing.

2. Snake and Devil Worshippers whose morality is to stay away from morality

3. Secular Humanist worshipping man's greatness with no moral guide whatsoever.

Speaking of morals, let's just say the whole guideline of Love your neighbor as yourself was not preached by God.

Let's also assume care for the poor, the homeless, the downtrodden, the sinner, was not taught by God.

Who in the world would not want the moral part of the Christian teachings JUST TO KEEP EVERYONE WORKING TOGETHER?

Instead of religious freedom as the founding fathers described, we are now trying to support the expansion of cults over religion. This is not only confusing the moral training of our children, but also it can be extremely dangerous. Our schools and government are both pushing what they call tolerance for Atheism, Satanism, Muslimism, and all the rest and forcing the Eliminate of "morality boosting prayer". Words like "In God We Trust" or even the holiday "Christmas" are considered violations of decent action in our schools and on our money. They don't mind spending "In God We Trust money, but just don't say it out loud and our Government is threatening you. If someone wants to wear a shirt saying something horrible like Happy Christmas, some students have been forced to turn their shirt backwards no matter how horrible it makes them feel. If someone brings in a shirt that says Love Kwanzaa, everyone cheers. This isn't even a religion but a Swahili word for "Praise the First Fruit of the Harvest". Who in the world would substitute a stupid Pear for God and think our government was going to be better.

Non-Christian Tolerance-Let's say a group decides to worship Satan and carry snakes in their pockets. Wanting to show "religious freedom", all students not liking the snakes become victims of the deviation. While there should be tolerance, we cannot disregard the fact that this is a deviation for normalcy to not be praised, highlighted, or put on a pedestal of greatness.

Satanist Tolerance-Here is what one Satanist "Britney Spears" once noted: "*To the untrained eye it might be difficult to differentiate between Satanists and Hippies. Both act pretentious, Satanists because they believe themselves their own Gods, Hippies because they think the Earth is their God. Both smell like rotting flesh, Hippies because* they don't bathe, Satanists because they eat rotten flesh. The main difference is that Satanists actually eat Hippies, and not vice versa." I know it's funny, but our country is tearing apart.

Moslem Tolerance-Let's say Moslems are allowed to do what is required in their sacred books. This would cause discomfort to others so it should be controlled. Here are a few "Holy" examples. While there should be tolerance, we cannot disregard the fact that this is a deviation for normalcy to not be praised, highlighted, or put on a pedestal of greatness.

Quran 22:19-22: "for them (Christian, Jews, and Hindu) garments of fire shall be cut and there shall be poured over their heads boiling water whereby whatever is in their bowels and skin shall be dissolved and they will be punished with hooked iron rods."
Quran 5:72- Christians will burn in the fire.
Rasul 553 "the Apostle of Allah said, 'Kill any Jew that falls into your power."
Quran 5:33- Allah said about apostates "they shall be killed or crucified or their hands and feet be cut off from the opposite sides

Bukhari 84:57 - 'Whoever changed his Islamic religion, kill him.'"

I know there are Muslims who don't go along with Muslimism, but many do and the ONLY way to get to their form of heaven and be serviced by virgins and boys is by following these teachings explicitly.

What is Going On?

If we look at the world population, we find the following:

86

- *33% - Believe in the saving God Jesus [love your Neighbor doctrine] [Christians]*
- *21%- Believe in the Moon God Allah' [Kill Christians doctrine][Muslims]*
- *2%- Believe in the Yahweh the Creator God [Only help Jews][Jews]*
- *14% Believe in the multi-headed Snake God [Reincarnation][Hindu]*
- *18%- Believe other tree and air gods [Isolation][Buddhist and nature religions]*
- *<1%- Believe in the Satan god [Evil wins out][Satanist]*
- *<1% Believe in Mother Nature God- Help plants not people][Witches/Wicca]*
- *<1%- Believe in Fruits of Harvest Gods [African Kwanza]*
- *10%- are Agnostic and believe there could be a God*
- *4%- are secular humanists and believe man is his own God.*

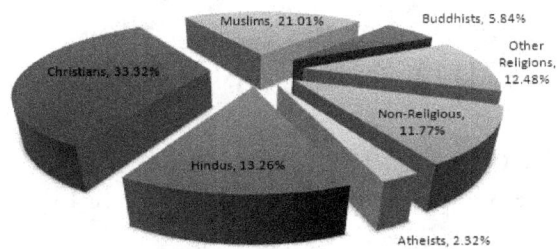

In the United States, it is even more telling as shown in the following graphic.
- *78% - Believe in the saving God Jesus [Christians]*
- *0.6%- Believe in the Moon God Allah' [Muslims]*
- *2%- Believe in the Yahweh the Creator God [Jews]*
- *0.4% Believe in the God Shiva [Hindu]*
- *1.6%- Believe other gods [Buddhist and nature religions]*

- *14%- are Agnostic and believe there could be a God*
- *2%- Believe man is his own God. [Humanists]*

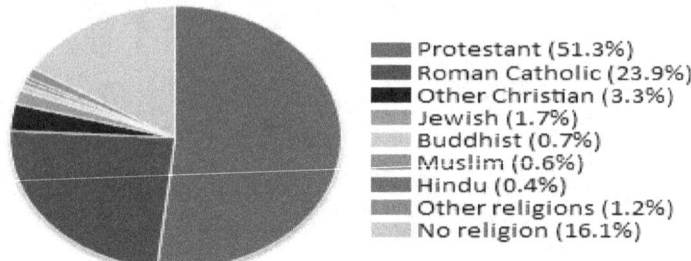

Protestant (51.3%)
Roman Catholic (23.9%)
Other Christian (3.3%)
Jewish (1.7%)
Buddhist (0.7%)
Muslim (0.6%)
Hindu (0.4%)
Other religions (1.2%)
No religion (16.1%)

*How can any nation build a system that can be sustained that **harms 98% of the students to coddle 2%?** What does that say about the worth of the Normal Americans????*

How dare schools and our government not let someone say a prayer anymore and let someone have Merry CHRISTMAS on their shirt anymore saying the holiday is not to Honor Christ, but to honor NOTHING. That is not only terribly unfair; it is one of the things pulling America down. How dare a government not allow a Christmas tree or Christmas party anymore, but allow for an atheist Kwanzaa demonstration in a SCHOOL. I'm not even getting into Eid ul Adha [The Muslim Christmas time celebration.] I don't know much about this Eid ul Adha, but I wonder what happens to effigies of Christians?

School Prayer Begins to be Outlawed

1962-The U.S. Supreme Court ruled that the Union Free School District No. 9 in Hyde Park, New York had violated the First Amendment by directing the Districts' principals to cause the following prayer to be said aloud by each class in the presence of a teacher at the beginning of each school day. *"Almighty God, we acknowledge our dependence upon*

Thee, and we beg Thy blessings upon us, our parents, our teachers and our Country."

1963-The U.S. Supreme Court banned school-directed recital of the Lord's Prayer and reading of Bible passages as part of *"devotional exercises"* in public schools.

1980-The U.S. Supreme Court *banned the posting of the Ten Commandments* on public school classroom walls.

1985-The U.S. Supreme Court banned observance of "daily moments of silence" from public schools when students were encouraged to pray during the silent periods.

Then it seems to turn around a little

1990-The U.S. Supreme Court held that schools must allow student prayer groups to organize and worship if other non-religious clubs are also permitted to meet on school property.

2000-The U.S. Supreme Court outlawed prayers led by members of the clergy at public school graduation ceremonies.

2000- Oops!! Supreme Court banned student-led pre-game prayers at public high school football games.

Why did this Happen?

Since 1962, the Supreme Court has consistently ruled that in *"Congress shall make no law respecting an establishment of religion,"* the Founding Fathers intended that "no" act of government (including public schools) should favor any one "religion" over others. That's hard to do, because once you mention God, Jesus, an 8 headed snake, the moon, peyote conjured wolves, the Devil, mother Nature or a tree, Darwin's evolution, and of course Kwanzaa's stupid Pear you have pushed the interpreted constitutional envelope by "favoring" one practice of religion over those of the majority and one that has the moral direction that can support holding our nation together.

Some have suggested that the only way to not favor one religion over others, is to not favor any religion at all or anything that some nut calls a religion. This appears to be the path now being chosen by many public schools—except for allowing the praise of pears, evolution, Mother Nature, Snakes, and the moon.

Just think about the Supreme Court's ruling against prayer—is that to protect Christianity or to insure it is not protected? How can our government make a stand against religion which is a violation of our Constitution?

Instead of being agnostic to religion,

- Our children are taught [Humanist quasi-religion] moral relativism in direct contradiction to Christianity. Before you start telling me this is not a religion, let me tell you it has been DEFINED as a religion by our new destructive government.

- They are taught [Evolutionist mutant sugars producing DNA religion] creation over creation in the self-image of God.

- They are being taught the Sexual cravings of the [Satanic "religion"]

- They are being pushed into Transvestism, Transsexualism, and I love my body and complete freedom religions.

- They have to turn their shirts inside out if they say anything about God like Merry Christmas.

Decisions like this are not the result of poor intellect. They are not the result of chance. They are not the result of mistakes. They are the result of cold calculation by elitists who want to turn your kids into serfs who serve only the state as an absence of a moral anchor will certainly allow others to easily mold our children to achieve power. Jesus said to render unto Caesar the things that are Caesar's and unto God the things that are God's. Do you think your children belong to Caesar?

Secular Humanism

As the soft sell Atheism this cult is increasing like wild fire since its inception in 1933. It is akin to Scientology, but more generalized. They accept Atheism as a character of their movement. Humanists have put together various Humanist Manifestos, in attempts to unify the Humanist identity. The original signers of the first Humanist Manifesto of 1933, declared themselves to be religious humanists. However, this "religion" did not profess a belief in <u>any god</u>. Now there are 5 branches of this infestation; "scientific", "ethical", "democratic", "religious", and "Marxist" humanism. Instead of being a religion, this cult believes the following: Humanism is a democratic and ethical life stance, which affirms that human beings have the right and responsibility to give meaning and shape to their own lives. They are their OWN GOD. On college campuses, 37 percent of men self-identified as "no religion" and 30 percent of women are also "nones" when asked about religion as they are becoming more and more Humanist. Let me ask a question. If no child is allowed to profess a moral compass or is threatened if he or she tries to show a religious attitude so that every evil is OK and tolerance, love, self- control are all taboo, what will the work ethic of the Millennials and later children be?

Bible and the Constitution

Proverbs 29:18-"*Where there is no vision, the people perish: but he that keeps the law is happy.*"

Proverbs 14:34- "*Righteousness exalts a nation: but sin is a reproach to any people.*"

Noah Webster quote "*It is extremely important to our nation, in a political as well as religious view, that all possible authority and influence should be given to the scriptures; for these furnish the best principles of civil liberty, and the most effectual support of republican government.*"

We have lost that support so our nation is crumbing before our eyes.

Increasing Moral Direction wil Reduce Drug use

This is an impossible thing to do, but we must try. Every year more and more drugs are found and flushed in an attempt at curbing this devastation. Much of the massive increase in incarceration is due to more and more drug arrests to support the same. Still the problem gets worse and worse. The first chart below shows a huge increase in prescription drugs starting about 1990 and the second chart shows the huge increase in in illegal drug arrests since 1975. While it seems like it has always been here. We can see it is only now getting too steep an incline to sustain our nation.

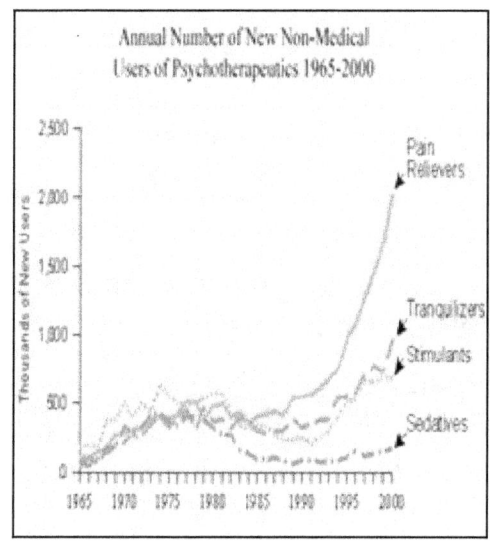

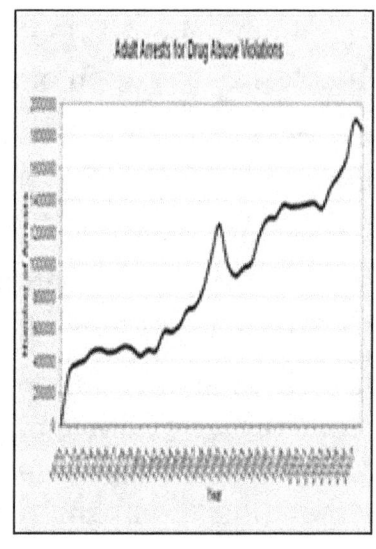

We understand that AIDS is an almost death sentence, so let's look at the statistics of people using the same needle and getting AIDS. What we see is that it is also a new problem and the problem has doubled since 1987.

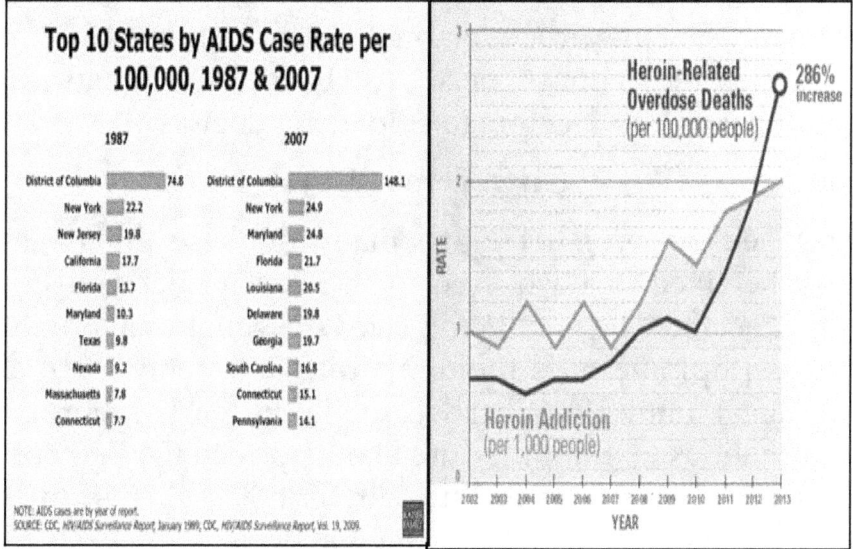

The last graph shows the death rate for heroin overdoses since 2002 has skyrocketed. Let me just ask one thing what is common about all of this? Recently everything in the drug world has gotten out of control

My personal belief is that these are symptoms of the following:

1. Loss of a moral direction and moral value fairly recently as anything goes without regard for tomorrow is pushed down our children's throat from middle school up.

2. Loss of family union expanded by the war on poverty making ½ of our country poverty slaves fairly recently. Families are spending less and less time with children so they find "companionship".

3. The inability to gain meaningful work recently as illegal immigrants take positions and any work received reduces money obtained by the government.

4. Inability to keep drugs out of our country as no one wants to secure our borders for same.

5. Advertisements from pharmaceutical companies to tell people they don't need to have ANY pain and willingness for Doctors to stop being doctors.

Girls Versus Boys

Don't get me wrong, I know many of these things can't easily be fixed, but we need to try. Let me let you in on another secret. The next graph shows psychotropic drug use of boys [top] and girls [bottom] from 2004 until 2014 and from age 1 until 17. What we see is that girls seem to be more cautious up until they are about 15 then they go crazy. Don't believe you sweet little girl is not giving in to this evil unless you are spending time with her

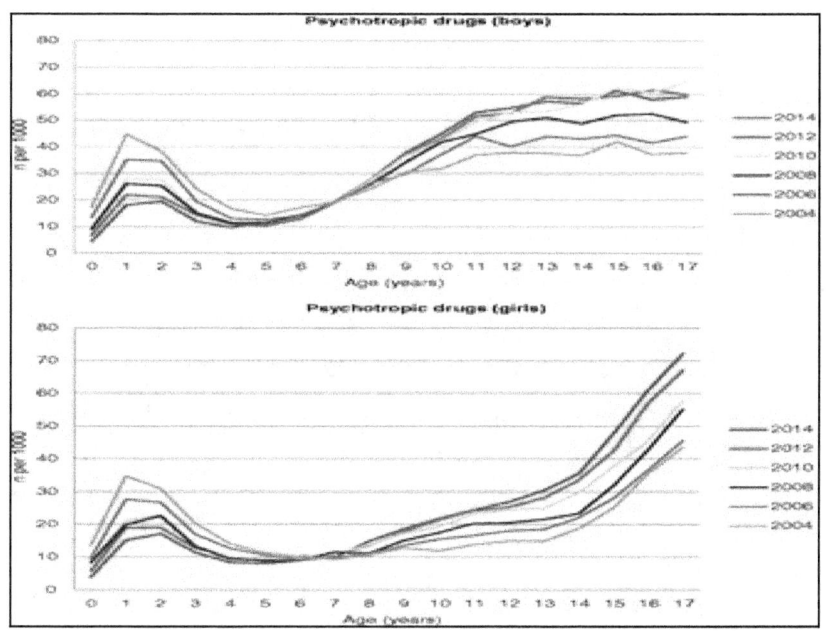

Outside of securing a moral direction, the biggest single antagonist for success in our country is something called slavery.

Eliminate Slavery

When I talk about slavery in this book, I'm not talking about the fact that in our earliest inception, America was loaded with 1/3 the population forced into slavery, nor am I talking about the Black slaves that followed. I'm not talking about the enslaved Chinese that built our railroad system nor the Native Americans enslaved by government support and "protection. The thing that is killing us today is still slavery, but it is a new kind. To understand, it might be good to review our history.

Slavery or the hatred that ensued because of this horrendous custom has gotten mixed up in our minds. We need to understand how it is addressed in the Constitution under what is called **General Welfare and pursuit of liberty**.

The colonists and many regions of the British Empire began to be flooded with a new commodity during the 17th century. This commodity was slaves. John Jay and many of the founding Fathers made strong strides in eliminating the custom even before the American Revolution, but by the time the 1st Constitution came about Slavery had been eliminated, but that is not the whole story as we try to envision the moral requirements for --*"Promoting the General Welfare and assuring Liberty for our Posterity."* While it began its fast rise to popularity in early 17th century America, we will find it continued until the time of Thomas Jefferson when importing slaves was outlawed under our 3rd Constitution in 1808. They were shackled, whipped, hung, dragged, and beaten into submission. If they tried to escape, they were hunted down and killed. No! I'm not talking about the black slaves; I'm talking about the white ones. The British continued to supply this commodity into the new world as they tried to "cleanse" their precious United Kingdom. When white slavery is acknowledged as having existed in America, it is almost always termed as "temporary indentured servitude" or part of the convict trade, by the way, there were not many in the temporary column. The "convicts" transported to America under the 1723 Waltham Act, perhaps numbered **100,000.** [Don't call them Slaves, but almost none became free in the land of the free!] To put this in perspective, the ENTIRE quantity of black slaves brought to the colonies over the entire 450 years of slave traffic was only 500 thousand. While the numbers are not accurately known, it is believed about 1.5 times that many criminal, indentured, and previously purchased white slaves were brought into the colonies over a much shorter timeframe. In the 1600s 1/3 of the population of the colonies was made up of white slaves. This quantity subsided a little. 1790 census there was about half a million slaves [about 16% of the total population in the United States]. This would include Black, Indian, and White as Chinese slaves had not yet entered the new nation. At least ½ of the slaves would have been white from the huge influx from the UK.

	1790 [Million]	1800 [M]	1840[M]
Slaves *	0.55	1.0	2.4
Free	3.5	5.6	14.6
Total in USA	4	6.6	17

These are black and white slaves [no separation is provided in the census between indentured, prisoner, *purchased or bred, white or black slaves. By 1840, the majority of slaves were black.]*The major use of white slaves began to reduce substantially in the 18th century, there were still white indentured slaves coming to America into the beginning of the 19th century. From Jay and other anti-slavery protester, *"Promoting the General Welfare and assuring Liberty for our Posterity"* could only be accomplished if all slaves could be part of the society. As I mentioned this would have included black men, but most of the slaves that Jay had come in contact with were the white slave factory workers in the northern States. There is a reason so many white slaves were here. They were cheaper than black slaves.

Cavanaugh on Irish Slaves

According to James Cavanaugh, author of *Irish Slaves of the Caribbean*, the English sold more Irish slaves between 1600 and 1699 than they did African slaves. **They were cheaper**, easier to offload, and ordered by the government. Cavanaugh indicated, *"The Proclamation of 1625 ordered that ALL Irish political prisoners be transported overseas and sold as "laborers" to English planters, who were settling the islands of the West Indies, officially establishing a policy that was to continue for two centuries. In 1629, a large group of Irish men and <u>women</u> were sent to Guiana, and by 1632, Irish were the <u>main slaves</u> sold to Antigua and Montserrat in the West Indies. But there were <u>not enough political prisoners to supply the demand</u>, so every petty infraction carried a sentence of transporting, and <u>slaver gangs combed the country sides to kidnap</u> enough people to fill out their quotas. In 1649, Cromwell landed in Ireland and attacked Drogheda, slaughtering some 30,000 Irish living in the city. Cromwell reported: 'I do not think 30 of*

98

their whole number escaped with their lives. <u>*Those that did are in safe custody in the Barbados.*</u>*"* I know this depiction is of those sold in the Islands below the colonies, but many also were sold to the other British colonies of the region. Shock of shocks! -----A few months later, in 1650, 25,000 Irish were sold in the Americas. Typical victims are shown below left.

White Child Slaves-During the 1650s decade of Cromwell's Reign of Terror, over <u>100,000 Irish children</u> were taken from Catholic parents and sold as slaves in the New Americas. [See above right]Tens of thousands of the White slaves were kidnapped children. To give you a feeling about the fear of your child being taken let's look at "English". The origin of the word "kidnapped" is kid-nabbed, the stealing of White children for enslavement. <u>The center of the trade in child-slaves was in the port cities of Britain and Scotland.</u> Many of the kid-nabbings were done by what were called "Press Gangs".

Kid-Nabbing-This segment comes from "Bound Over" by Van der Zee. *"**Press gangs** in the hire of local merchants roamed the streets, seizing 'by force such boys as seemed proper subjects for the slave trade.' Children were driven **in flocks** through the town and confined for shipment in barns...So flagrant was the practice that people in the countryside about Aberdeen avoided bringing children into the city for fear they might be stolen; and so widespread was the collusion of merchants, shippers, suppliers and* *even magistrates that the man who exposed it was forced to recant and run out of town."* Once the children were in the new world, some went to the factories as shown below.

The indentured servants, who served a tidy little period of 7 years polishing the master's silver and china and then taking their place in colonial high society, were <u>a minuscule fraction</u> of the great unsung hundreds of thousands of White slaves who were worked to death in this country from the early 17th century onward. Up to <u>one-half of all the initial arrivals in the American colonies were white slaves</u> and they were America's first slaves. These figures tell us that the 1st Constitution elimination of Slavery was to mostly halt white slavery. These white humans were almost always slaves for life, long before black Africans became more prominent. This slavery was even hereditary. White children born to White slaves were enslaved too. Whites were auctioned on the block with children sold and separated from their parents and wives sold and separated from their husbands. Free black property owners were on the streets of northern and southern American cities while White slaves were worked to death in the sugar mills of Barbados and Jamaica and the plantations of Virginia, so let's not forget that slavery was awful no matter what color someone happened to be.

It has been estimated that ninety percent of the White slavery in America was conducted without indentures of any kind but according to the so-called "custom of the country". Many places in the North American colonies, the custom was almost always continued servitude after the indenture. During the 1650s, over 100,000 Irish children between the ages of 10 and 14 were taken from their parents and sold as slaves in the West Indies, Virginia and New England. In 1656, Cromwell ordered that 2,000 Irish children be taken to the Americas and sold as slaves to English settlers. During this same time, 52,000 Irish (mostly women and children) were sold to Barbados and Virginia. Another 30,000 Irish men and women were also transported and sold to the highest bidder. You can imagine why so many women were among those sold. There is no doubt that in 17th century colonial America and on both sides of the Atlantic, white slavery was a far more extensive operation than Black enslavement. In the beginning of the 18th century, there were more white slaves and in the later part there were beginning to be a higher percentage of black slaves. Even during the latter part of the 18th century there was kidnapping of Anglo-Saxons into slavery as well as convict slavery.

Proclamation of 1625-The Irish slave trade began when James II sold 30,000 Irish prisoners as slaves to the New World. His Proclamation of 1625 required Irish political prisoners be sent overseas and sold to English settlers in the West Indies. By the mid-1600s, the Irish were the main slaves sold to Antigua and Montserrat. At that time, 70% of the total population of Montserrat were Irish slaves. Ireland quickly became the ***biggest source of human livestock*** for English merchants. Again let me say it once more; the majority of the early slaves to the New World were white. Irish were the main country of export, initially because of religion and then simply because they were not considered human. From 1641 to 1652, <u>over 500,000 Irish were killed by the English and another 300,000 were sold as slaves</u>. Ireland's population fell from about <u>1,500,000 to 600,000 in one single decade</u>.

Bacon's Rebellion-Some of these slaves were eventually freed but by 1660, much of the best land was claimed by the large land owners. The former servants were pushed westward, where the mountainous land was less arable and the threat from Indians constant. A class of angry, impoverished pioneer farmers began to emerge as the 1600s grew old. After the Indentured Servant War called Bacon's Rebellion in 1676, planters began to prefer permanent African slavery to the headright system that had previously enabled them to prosper. *"Packed Densely, Like Herrings": Gottlieb Mittelberger Warned His Countryman of the Perils of Emigration, 1750.*

A Description of German Slave Transport-In the early eighteenth centuries, many colonists arrived as indentured servants or bondsmen. This practice meant that impoverished Germans and other Europeans financed their passage across the Atlantic. Between 1749 and 1754 more than 30,000 Germans came to Pennsylvania, and by mid-century they constituted about one third of the colony's population. Both in Rotterdam and in Amsterdam the people are packed densely, like herrings so to say, in the large sea-vessels. One person receives a place of scarcely 2 feet width and 6 feet length in the bedstead, while many a ship carries four to six hundred souls; not to mention the innumerable implements, tools, provisions, water-barrels and other things which likewise occupy such space.

When the ships have for the last time weighed their anchors near the city of Kaupp in Old England, the real misery begins with the long voyage. For from there the ships, unless they have good wind, must often sail 8, 9, 10 to 12 weeks before they reach Philadelphia. But even with the best wind the voyage lasts 7 weeks. But during the voyage there is on board these ships terrible misery, stench, fumes, horror, vomiting, many kinds of sea-sickness, fever, dysentery, headache, heat, constipation, boils, scurvy, cancer, mouth rot, and the like, all of which come from old and sharply salted food and meat, also from very bad and foul water, so that many die miserably. Add to this want of provisions, hunger, thirst, frost, heat, dampness, anxiety, want, afflictions and lamentations, together with other trouble, as . . . the lice abound so frightfully, especially on sick people, that they can be scraped off the body. The misery reaches the climax when a gale rages for 2 or 3 nights and days, so that everyone believes that the ship will go to the bottom with all human beings on board. In such a visitation the people cry and pray most piteously. Children from 1 to 7 years rarely survive the voyage. I witnessed . . . misery in **no less than 32 children in our ship, all of whom were thrown into the sea.** The parents grieve all the more since their children find no resting-place in the earth, but are devoured by the monsters of the sea. The water which is served out of the ships is often very black, thick and full of worms, so that one cannot drink it without loathing, even with the greatest thirst. Toward the end we were compelled to eat the ship's biscuit which had been spoiled long ago; though in a whole biscuit there was scarcely a piece the size of a dollar that had not been full of red worms and spiders' nests. . . .

Before we could begin to eliminate the new push for black slaves, the trade of white slaves had to be eliminated. I know this is not a fair statement, but it provides the sentiment of the Revolutionaries. The first constitution had generally outlawed slavery, but the second one seemed to reinstitute the horror. people did not turn around in the 2nd Constitution and want slavery again, they simply had changed focus on eliminating ALL slaves [including black slaves] and it would be an uphill battle. Let's review a little about black slaves. While most know more of this segment, we still should address it as it was a horrible custom.

Black Slavery

While we are talking about slavery, many already know white people were not the only slaves in America. We had better look at the cause of General Welfare and Pursuit of liberty when it comes to the black slave populations that would soon overtake the White slaves. Black slavery was much worse in its devaluing of humanity. While Andrew Johnson was able to bring himself up from white slavery to become President and possible Samuel Huntington did a similar unbelievable task, no black Chinese or American Indian Slaves Every were able to even be considered for the position. These non-white slaves were considered to be less civilized and even less human. Here are just a few of the examples from Abraham Lincoln, the Supreme Court, and 13th Amendment to the Constitution that was replaced after the 4th Civil War that show this horrible sentiment.

Supreme Court Decision [1857]-"*The question before us is, whether [Negroes] ... compose a portion of [the American] people and are constituent members of this* *sovereignty? We think they are not.... On the contrary, they [are] ... **a subordinate and inferior class of beings**, who [have] been subjugated by the dominant race.... [They] can therefore claim none of the rights and privileges which [the Constitution] provides for ... citizens of the United States."*

Senator Abraham Lincoln Address [1858]-*"I will say then that I am not, nor ever have been, in favor of bringing about in any way the **social and political equality of the white and black races**. I am not, nor ever have been, in favor of making **voters or jurors of Negroes, nor of qualifying them to hold office**, nor to **intermarry with white people**. I will say in addition to this that there is a physical difference between the white and black races which I believe will forever forbid the **two races living together on terms of social and political equality**. And inasmuch as they cannot so live, while they do remain together there must be the position of superior and inferior and I as much as any other man am in favor of having **the superior position assigned to the white race**.*

Corwin's 13th Amendment [1861]-This amendment was pushed by Lincoln, and passed both houses and had already been ratified by a few States as the 4th Civil War of our country began. Here is the sentiment of the Nation. *No amendment shall be made to the Constitution which will authorize or give to Congress the power to abolish or interfere, within any State, with the domestic institutions thereof, <u>including that of persons held to labor or service</u> by the laws of said State."*

As I mentioned before, the English and French black slave trade occurred between 1450 and 1900. While the yearly number of black slaves purchased in the colonies was fairly low, one can see from the sentiment of the nation that their lot was horrible. If you are wondering just how many Black slave POWs were exported from Africa, during this 450 year period there were <u>over 11 Million Africans</u> that were transported around the world. Here's the part to remember with respect to American History. <u>Only 4% of them were sold to the colonists</u> that would soon be called the United States. The rest found their way to other, not so pleasant, areas. It seemed like Africans were trying to destroy Africa during this terrible age. Just as one group would win one war and take away slaves, another group would beat the winning group and they would become slaves themselves. This was the African form of genocide and it was substantially different that Hitler's. Instead of killing the losers, the winners made money with them and still accomplished the same genocide. There was no reason to have huge prisons or even huge execution areas. This slave thing made warring easy and efficient. The groups that made out the most from the Africans killing each other and driving each other into slavery were the English and the French.

Outlawed in 1808-Only 500 thousand African slaves were brought to the United States colonies over the entire 450 years of the African slave trade. All the rest were born in the United States. <u>President Jefferson had outlawed the practice of receiving slaves from another country in 1808</u> so most of the depictions of slave-ships continually coming to North America carrying sardine packed slaves is not a complete picture. The percentage of white and black slaves to non-slaves was continuously decreasing in the United States before the United States' 4th Civil War of 1862. As shown below, the slave population was <u>18% of the total population in 1800</u> [not including those classified as

106

indentured servants] and the percentage had dropped to only 13% by 1860.

Slave Use Growth	1800	1810	1840	1860
Slaves north [M]	.2	.2	.4	.4
Free north [M]	3	3.8	9.6	20.3
Slaves south [M]	.7	.9	2	3.2
Free south [M]	1.2	1.8	5	7
% slaves north	6%	6%	4%	2%
% slaves south	35%	33%	30%	31%

For those thinking the North and South ideals were substantially different we should note that the drop was about the same in both north and south with about a 4% drop in percentage of slave population experienced in both the north and south during this period. Certainly, there were more slaves in the Agrarian sections of the country, but the thing to look at here was that the numbers were going down. According to the 1860 census, there were over 130 thousand free black Americans living in the various "rebellion" States before the war started [about 3.5% of the black population]. While that number is appallingly low, it was getting larger every year as slavery was becoming a thing of the past. Here is a question, what State outlawed slavery first? You guessed it Georgia was the first to outlaw it in 1733, but the law was repealed within a year when the crops needed to come in, I suppose. By events of the war and normal consequence, black slavery eventually ended, but it still would take a long time for black Americans to be given the same consideration as white Americans. During the 1904 World's Fair a number of African exhibits showed the backwardness and less than civilized nature of the Africans and many Americans came to view this type of zoo as shown below left.

That brings us to the African pigmy named Ota Benga shown right. In 1906 he is well known as being the last African placed on display at the Bronx Zoo as the missing link. To add effect, Ota had a chimpanzee that he would carry and a small bow and arrow which he used to shoot at visitors. Finally, black Americans began feeling the freedoms of other Americans, but something called the "War on Poverty" would almost destroy that freedom. Right now let's continue with another slave population. This one was not freed with the Emancipation Proclamation.

Yellow Slaves

California was an important State for a number of reasons. Not only was San Francisco becoming one of the largest towns in the country, but more importantly, a new breed of slaves was erupting that would begin to weaken the control of the Industrialist States if nothing was done. These "slaves" were from China and they were unique. They worked harder than black slaves and they were NOT CALLED slaves. Certainly, they were beaten if they ran off, were segregated from Normal Americans, were required to work longer hours than normal people, were not allowed to marry and have children, were not allowed to own land, and were not allowed to stake a claim for gold or minerals, but they were sort-of paid for their services [less than a third of a Normal person] so no one had to say they were slaves. Anyone with half a brain would have recognized that this new type of slave would soon be instituted and the "slave substitute" in the slave States to increase production and to eliminate the slave stigma. If that happened, the mid-western agrarian States would not be able to be controlled by the Industrialist statettes [super tiny States that still got exactly the same number of Senators as a normal or huge State] and larger States in Congress as farmers would vote with farmers if the slave issue had been settled.

By far the major reason that black slave laborers were not the primary method for establishing the transcontinental Railroad was the Chinese labor force. The main reason that California had no "black" slaves and became a "free state" was this very same super cheap, beat-me, abuse-me labor force. They worked for practically nothing, worked harder than almost any slave, they complained less, and the typically didn't talk to anyone outside their own community. Who needed slaves with Chinese around? By 1860, almost 10% of the population of California was Chinese "quasi-slave-workers".

Chinese Were not Slaves-While we are on this subject that I'm staying out of let me say that the thousands of Chinese working on the railroad systems were in no way slaves. Yes, they were whipped if they tried to leave the railroad site and the white workers of the railroads were paid about 300% times the average Chinese "salary". But that doesn't mean anything. Oh yes, the white workers on the railroads had box car housing while the "non-slave" Chinese had to survive in tents or nothing at all and these same Chinese were <u>considered to be less than human</u>. All this can be twisted out of proportion. After all, <u>the employers were the ones who were championing "anti-slavery"</u>. The images show the whipping, working without shoes, and tent housing in extremely cold snow conditions.

Don't even think they were enslaved. Ha!

So the question might be how did farmers exist after the Civil War? Well they used slaves of course, but they had more efficient ones in the form of Chinese. After the Emancipation Proclamation, Chinese rushed to fill the worker spots as <u>unfortunate black Americans now had no place to go</u>. Chinese in droves went to Arkansas and Louisiana, to work on plantations. Almost immediately after the Civil Right Act of 1870, the <u>Chinese gained the freedom of marriage</u>. The 1870 U.S. census of Louisiana showed a massive marrying rush with well over ½ of all Chinese marriages to black women so there was some carryover of black slavery, I suppose.

Initially entering the United States in the 1790s, once they got here they became the new version of Slave in California. By 1880, there were still well over 300 thousand Chinese still in California even with horrible treatment that left many dead. Here are some of the basic characteristics of this new commodity, that we shall not call slaves.

They were classified as sub-human and not allowed the services of the law hold office or even be on a jury [see below]

They could not own land and could not become citizens []

They could not marry white women [Naturalization Act 1790 and Anti-Miscegenation Laws]

Laws were passed to exclude Chinese immigration of women that could increase the control of the Chinese and make their lives less burdensome. [Chinese Exclusion Act and Geary Act- not eliminated until 1924]

They were [usually] paid a small amount [1/10th of the "Normal" workers] by railroads, and consisted of 90% of the Worker/slave base. Beaten, chained, and not provided any housing, they were killed by the dozens in landslides, and explosions as they were forced to punch holes through mountainsides, but they still were paid so the 13th Amendment was not violated exactly.

They had to pay "special taxes of $3 per day under the "Foreign Miners Tax Act" if they wished to dig for minerals. [Average money obtained was $6 per month- Many fake tax collectors came collected additional tax, burned settlements, and drove Chinese away from mines without and redress by the law. This law lasted until 1870.]*

Chinese and the Supreme Court-This was before the Dred Scot decision that black slaves were not Americans. In 1854 the California Supreme Court, decided, the Chinese were sub human [Slaves] with no legal rights. Let's see what they said.

*They are-- a race of people whom nature has marked as inferior, and who **are incapable of progress or intellectual development** beyond a certain point, as their history has shown; **differing in color, and physical conformation;** between whom and ourselves nature has placed an impassable difference and as such had **no right to swear** away the life of a citizen or participate with us in administering the affairs of our Government. "*

These slaves were not even allowed to testify as witnesses before the court against white citizens, including those accused of murder. Their "masters" could do and did whatever they wanted and the courts would not even hear a claim. Forget the Emancipation Proclamation for Blacks, This ruling lasted MUCH LONGER [until 1873] and somehow went around the 13th Amendment of 1863 making emancipated slaves Americans. Like the black slave horrors, this ruling effectively made white violence against Chinese Americans unprosecutable, as they had now no possibility to assert their rightful legal entitlements or claims – possibly in cases of theft or breaches of agreement – in court. The ruling remained in force until 1873. Black, White, and Yellow men were all losing the war on General Welfare and the pursuit of Liberty for their children. Just as things began to turn around President Johnson came along and started what many call the "War to Poverty". The next group is the Red people, while the actions were somewhat different; there is a limitation that should be addressed.

While many settlers left the eastern coast to find gold, and adventure, some simply had to leave. It was getting so bad in the Industrialist Northeast that many of the American inhabitants were almost forced to go west. Initially the people of the Civil War era began migrating towards the industrialist centers of our country only to find out it was not wonderful for the workers. The living conditions were unbearable, the wages were less than adequate, and the work was hard and long, mostly being accomplished by indentured and the destitute. Out of desperation, our inhabitants went a new direction to find general welfare and liberty. With all of the new weapons designed for the Civil War and the Vanderbilt railroads, this group of Americans quickly took over the area that was once owned by the American Indians. For centuries it was common practice for Indian tribes to completely annihilate one tribe and then another tribe would annihilate the victors. It was their accepted way of life. This new annihilation would come from "outsiders". As the settlers moved in, the Indians were slaughtered, moved, and ALMOST forgotten.

Only Red People Should Kill Red People-Many people today feel that the white people had no business killing red people. Only red people were supposed to kill red people, or at least, that is what red people told them. Our schools even promoted the unfair notion that white people killed "defenseless" red people. While there is reason to believe that this was done in some cases like the case identified with Abraham Lincoln and his mass execution of the Sioux, our schools go overboard. I heard it continuously. "We should be ashamed for the actions of those slaughtering marauders", they continue to teach, "--and if we were really ashamed, we should give the remaining Indians special privileges like not having to live by our Constitution and law, building casinos where Americans were not allowed, not paying taxes and killing eagles when it was forbidden to Americans. If those nasty white, yellow, and black people do the things that are restricted for Indians, we need to put them in prison. After all, the terrible white, yellow, and black people killed Indians over a hundred years ago and their skin color isn't right." OK! Some of the actual words are not expressed, but the crazy sentiment is there just the same.

If any of the people who are <u>against</u> giving black skinned Americans money [Reparations] because their ancestors were slaves during and before the four Civil Wars and believe that the American Indians are somehow different and <u>should</u> get special reparations, I feel sorry for them.

While I'm on this subject, let's think about this whole Indian reparations thing in some reasonable light. These crazy and debilitating reparations go as far as giving away huge blocks of land. Some of these blocks of land or <u>reservations</u> are larger than some of our States, all of these areas together only <u>hold a population of about 1½ %</u> of the "regular American" population, and our laws don't apply to these people in these block of land. Let's call them what they are- **"Indian Countries"**. For those who haven't counted them, there are **588 of these countries INSIDE our borders.**

Post War Indian Countries-From the chart below, notice that all our cities and residential areas for 98.5% of the people only add up to 4.3% of the land that makes up the United States or 98 million acres. This is about ***0.3 acres per person*** and business. The vast majority of the land is "secret land" where no living, working, residential-ing, or urbanizing is done. That is another story not covered in this book. The remaining 1.5% of the "quasi American, red-people" get 56 million acres or ***12.5 acres per person*** given to them <u>rent free, tax free, and almost law free</u>. Yes, I'm talking mean about the American Indians.

	Acres [M]	% of Total
Not Indian, business, or residential land	2127	93.2%
Non-Indian Residential and Business Land. 98% of the people live work and die on this part of the United States.	98	4.3%
Indian Reservations [1.5% of the people]	56	2.5%

The strange thing is that it isn't just one piece of land. It is hundreds of pieces. The American Government sends money to the residents. That might be OK if we got something for our money or if we were doing it for our citizens, but these people are above some of the laws that people who are not getting free land and yearly payments must abide by. Certainly, the "freedom" everyone knows is that these countries can have gambling inside their countries regardless of what the laws of the country are. Everyone has also heard about how these above the law quasi-citizens can also kill American Eagles without the normal repercussions. There are 304 different types of "reservation living groups" that are treated in this special way and given countries inside the United States Boundaries. <u>Twenty one of the blocks of land are larger than the State of Rhode Island</u>. Several are larger than 3 or 4 of the Northeastern Statettes so sometimes we are talking about huge pieces of land. Other plots of land are small where a special group decided that they liked a different area than the large Indian countries. Remember we are talking about 588 pieces of land scattered all over the place. [That's 588 internal

115

countries that live outside our law, but with HUGE foreign aid].

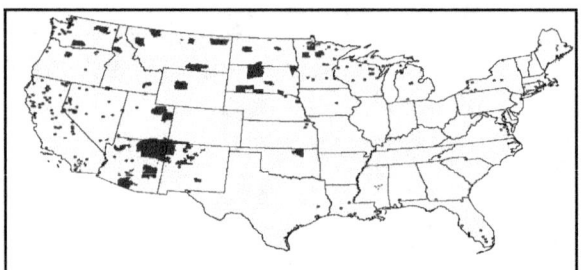

The picture above shows the 422 "country-ettes" that are scattered around the main portion of our country and no one seems to care. Many of the land areas are worth substantial amounts of money, especially the 83 country-ettes inside the State of California. These guys don't pay Federal, State income taxes or even sales taxes if they have business dealing inside their countries, but we pay them money every year to keep them enslaved. This is wrong.

A Quick History-Here's the deal. Hundreds of years ago and these guys lost a war. Rather than simply moving, they used horrible terrorist tactics to continue the insanity that are simply too horrible to discuss. If we go back a little, the Before the Europeans came; the Adena lost a war with the Ronnongwetowanca people rules most of North America until they were slaughtered by the Adena. These red people lasted until the Aztalan people annihilated them. These people ruled until the Hopewell annihilated them. On and on massacre after genocidic massacre; even if they would have had compassion on the losers, they would not have given them free land for hundreds of years and treated them as if they were better than themselves by not taxing them and still providing them money so they would not have to work.

Burial Mounds-In the Ohio Valley, the Adena people buried the Ronnongwetowanca under massive human filled hills as shown below. Later Indians would bury the Adena and Aztalan the same way.

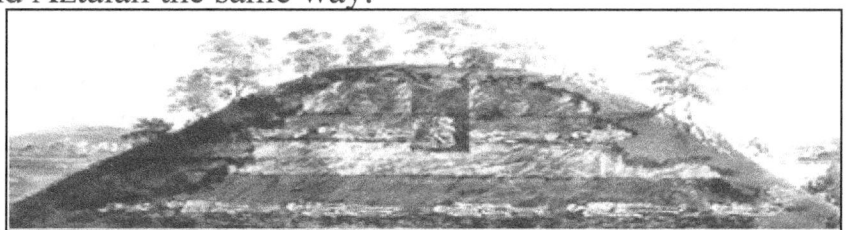

Example Battle-In Wichita, Kansas was found the greatest prehistoric battle and burying ground yet discovered in the United States has just been found near the little town of Redlands. Here they discovered what appear to be nearly 100,000 warriors who met death in battle. With nearly 3,000 skeletons to every square acre, they were able to dig out, by the carload, hundreds of skulls and skeletons showing the signs of battle; some with as many as five arrow points sticking into it. Maybe we should take the American Indian example and quit supporting these other countries **OR** make these guys REAL citizens of the United States. When Polish people come to America, they don't get to have their own country and neither do the Mexicans. Ok! We will get to them shortly.

Either eliminate the "Indian Countries" [reservations] and don't give them continuing aid or make the Indians real citizens.

Here is what we have done to the Red people. These people are probably some of the poorest quasi-Americans you can imagine simply because of these hand-outs. What we are doing is a horrible and unjust thing that goes against the Constitution. [I know there is an amendment that says we have to, but that MUST be changes ASAP.]

Stop foreign Aid to reservation immediately-Italy isn't still paying Etruscans for taking their land. England doesn't pay the Vikings. The Cherokee Indians don't even pay the ancient Hopewell, Azatlan, Adena, or the Ronnongwetowanca [also known as the Archaics] that were almost annihilated to allow for Cherokee expansion. No nation practices such absurdity. It is simply wrong and historians seem to ignore the injustice simply because the American Indians are portrayed as a victim still after hundreds of years.

Let's not hide behind the facts. ---Today we spend about $1.5 Billion dollars a year in foreign aid to the Indian countries under what is called the Bureau of Indian Affairs.

Even with that, the Indians are provided assistance from other non-Indian assistance and welfare programs including those from the Oklahoma Indian Welfare Act and others. About 50% of the 1.8 million Indians in the United States live inside the Indian Reservation/countries where each family member including children are essentially given about 60 acres of land without charge. To top it off, we gave them back the right to vote outside their country without requiring them to conform to the laws of the United States.

Rich Indians-By the way, not all Indians are poor in fact many are extremely wealthy. If we were to classify the richest set of American Indians, it would be the Aguas Calientes of Palm Springs. While there are less than 200 individuals in this destitute tribe, the land "held by tribal trust" is worth over $1.5 Billion dollars. It seems there has been no reasonable study on the wealth of Indians to show that they, as a group, no longer need or should get our support. As long as individual Indians don't have a reasonable way of distributing wealth and many stay in abject poverty, we will continue to feel guilty.

Sickness

While we are on the subject of feeling guilty about Indians let me say that the red man was killed more by virulent diseases than any disruption of Indian society, or by war, or American intervention. Let me just provide you with a simple timeline of the major epidemics affecting Native Americans. Certainly, these affected all Americans, but this section is on Indians and they fared far worse than the general population.

Bubonic Plagues-The first wave was from 1613until 1617, Bubonic Plague halved Florida's native population. Again it hit in 1619 and 20, killing 60 to 80% of the New England natives Pilgrims survived their first winter because of this plagues as entire villages were wiped out and blankets, food, and shelter all were left behind. [Don't think of them as grave robbers; just think of them as survivors living because of the dead Indians.]

Measles- Like the bubonic plague, measles hit hard. 1633-34, measles killed up to 50% of New England and Great Lakes natives. In 1658-59, it struck hard again. In 1692-93 it struck again. In 1713-15 it struck New England and Great Lakes peoples. By 1727-28 it spread across the continent. In 1768-69 measles struck southwestern U.S. peoples and in 1776-78 it spread from Texas to Hudson Bay. Each time, huge quantities of Indians met their end.

Malaria- Malaria was not as bad but in 1695-96 malaria killed large quantities of Native Americans.

Scarlet Fever-1637-38, Scarlet Fever killed large quantities of New England & Great Lakes natives

Influenza- The common flu came along as well. In 1647-48, influenza killed large quantities of Native Americans. Again in 1675-76 it again killed large quantities of Native Americans. It struck another blow 1761-62 as it spread across North America

Diptheria- In1659-60, Diptheria killed large quantities of Native Americans. In 1735-36 it became epidemic among New England tribes

Smallpox-Smallpox is the all-time leader and still champion. This was the most devastating and wide reaching epidemic disease to affect North America. In 1649-50, Smallpox killed large quantities of Native Americans. In 1639-40 it killed large quantities in New England. In 1633-34 it killed large quantities in Great Lakes. In 1662-63 it killed large quantities of Native Americans. In 1669-70 it killed large quantities of Native Americans. In 1687-88 it killed another large group of Native Americans. In 1715-21 it spread at least from Texas to New England. In 1729-30 it swept across the continent again. In 1738-39 it went from Texas to Hudson Bay. In 1750-51 it went from Texas to the Great Lakes again. In 1755-56 it killed some more. In 1765-66 we found more dead. In 1779-81 smallpox moved over all North America again. In 1786-87 it was felt in Alaska and Canada. In 1788-89 the disease came to the Pueblo Indians. In 1815-16 it hit the Pueblo and Plains Indians. In 1831-34 it greatly affected Plains and Great Lakes tribes. In 1836-40 it killed native peoples of Alaska & Pueblos. In 1843-46 it killed many Aleut to the Plains peoples More were killed during the following dates 1848-50, 1852-53, 1854-57, 1866-67, 1876-78, and in 1897-99.

So many Indians died, the non-red Americans decided they should be given their own little countries as restitution.

Sure there were some that were killing in the 100 years Indian Wars, but that was a small fraction compared to disease. The Indians were already dead and on their way to extinction. The major portions of the Indian nations had already been defeated by disease. This whole Indian guilt thing is nonsense. Non-red Americans were not the major cause of the misery and even if they contributed by unintentionally carrying germs, the whole concept seems twisted. I know this section does not sound like Red Men were not slaves, but they were enslaved by the very thing that is enslaving many populations in the United States today. Called Welfare, there is no welfare in it. Called subsistence, it only yanks people away from hope and pushes them into the bowels of welfare despair living only at the whim of the government. Once Indians become Americans again, we can get them out of the slave-making-poverty. This will cost less money and make our country stronger.

Establish Jobs not Slavery

While the specific institute of slavery is supposedly gone from Black, White, Red, and yellow people, we find it is not gone. For a time, there was hope until Lyndon Johnson came up with something he called "War On Poverty" [1965]. It actually was a war to secure poverty and the enslavement of people forced into this predicament. Sure there were bad times and good times before Johnson came along, so we can't blame all of our misery on him, but he did a number on us and we are falling farther and farther away from general welfare and the elimination of poverty slaves every year.

Quotas of Immigration

Even if we start to control, limit, reduce and eliminate illegal entry of foreigners that exceeds the quotes set to protect us, we still have another serious problem that limits and generally eliminates any action to provide the General Welfare that is something we can call the establishment of government slavery and more and more become totally dependent on the government.

How can we Eliminate this Slavery?-One thing to do is we must eliminate the Earned Income Credit, free day care, free housing, free lunch, free food stamps, free phones, and free medical handouts **as they are currently established**. I'm certainly not saying we should not provide those funds to insure domestic tranquility and reduction in lawlessness as required in the Constitution, but the funds cannot be given to those not working. Instead, welfare payments MUST be given to industry in some way with the stipulation and restriction that funds are for hiring those not working and to allow for a low cost workforce to be trained. This could be done by tax credit, earned income credit to a company, or many things that would not even cost up-front money. I know it sounds simple, but there would not be as many kickbacks so someone would truly need to make a pledge to govern in accordance to our Constitution rather than the corrupt form we have let ourselves accept.

This redistribution of "welfare dollars" would allow free or nearly free **American Manpower** from people who are desperately trying to find work and push themselves towards freedom. By not being enslaved by the government directly the system would build confidence, establish a place of learning, generate more community awareness, build country patriotism, and ---over time—allow those needing opportunity to pursue liberty that goal and vision while REDUCING the cost of supporting our population.

By working for the money they spend on medical, food, daycare, housing, and survival, these Americans can begin to increase their confidence, increase pride in their country, increase possibility of sustained livelihood away from government assistance and a large portion will soon be on their own if the program was run in an appropriate way.

The chart below shows how Roosevelt's stuff began a huge cost in what we now call welfare payments. Notice that when Truman got elected, just about all these things were eliminated. When Johnson came into power we began a spiral of death and we began losing the war on poverty in something he laughingly called the "War on Poverty".

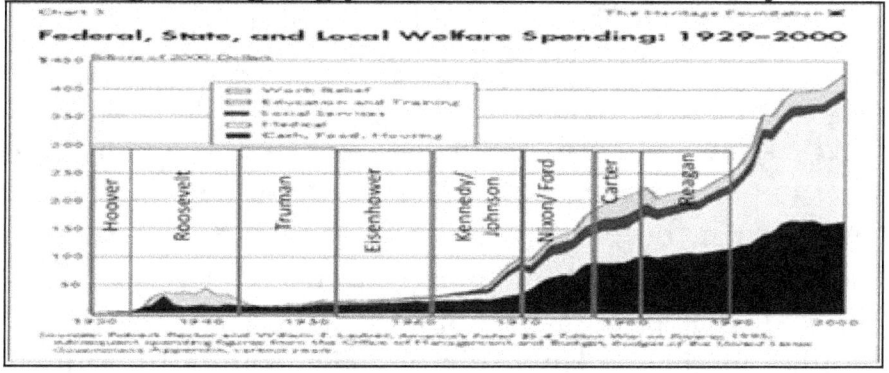

Eliminate Glamorized Poverty

On a similar note, we must eliminate the glamorization of poverty. Given 2 choices getting money for nothing or getting money for work, some will pick the first one. OK!

Many will as we see every day as there is no stigma for not working.

There is no stigma for poverty for poverties sake at all. Those on food stamps buy almost any type of food they want. Certainly minimum daily food substance should be provided, especially to children, but the food should be provided by rigid adherence providing most of this support by leftover food stuff, and mass quantity cereals that provide this limited subsistence without the desire for poor to use this program to buy expensive steaks or put their families on food stamps to cover their smoking, drinking, or drug habits. These things are becoming an encouragement to not work. They allow desperate people to slip into the Slavery of the welfare State. Some indicate we cannot embarrass the poor and I believe that is a truth provided they are doing whatever they can to eliminate this state.

In the previous example I presented that showed a woman working part time at $29,000 per year made more money that a woman making $69,000 per year if both had 2 children to care for. There is a certain glamor to that whole thing--the life of "freedom from work". Instead of paying direct payments to provide this same service, wouldn't it be better to provide funding to an industry so the poor woman could have a decent full time job and training for some time, bring her up to something near the $69,000 wage for a time, have her pay for those things she needs and not give the other mother a slap in the face for working full time to take care of her family?

Discouraged from Finding Work- If you want to jeopardize our General Welfare the most, simply discourage people from finding work. Bringing in foreigners to work to limit jobs not only reduces the jobs available, but also limits jobs by artificially increasing salaries of second tier jobs so that only those well qualified can get them. I know this sounds backwards, but even while jobs are fading those in technical positions still are doing well. There are at least **almost 100 different federal programs** designed to _"help"_ _lower-income_ Americans as shown below that added up to a trillion dollars in 2012 and is still increasing. The problem is they all do the opposite eliminate freedom, reduce our workforce and stifle the welfare of our country.

Program Area	# of federal programs	Cost in FY2012
Cash aid	5	$250 billion
Education and job training	28	$100 billion
Energy	2	$5 billion
Food aid	17	$150 billion
Health care	8	$300 billion
Housing	22	$50 billion
Social Services	8	$15 billion
Veterans	2	$25 billion
TOTALS	92	$1 trillion

There are dozens of education and job-training programs which could help if they were run right. There are 17 different food-aid programs and over 20 housing programs. Just imagine what a $ trillion dollars could do for our country in ACTUALLY establishing the GENERAL Welfare.

Just how Much has Johnson's Poverty Fiasco Cost?

If we just take the money spent over the last 50 years since Johnson's failed *"war on poverty"* started, U.S. taxpayers have spent over $22 trillion on the anti-constitutional promote-poverty programs. Let me give you a comparison.

*Once adjusted for inflation, this spending (**not including Social Security or Medicare**) is three times the cost of all U.S. military wars since the American Revolution.*

Here are the major elements of his unthinking, unproductive, country destroying, Poverty slave making, and government overreach programs.

125

- **The Social Security Amendments of 1965**- created Medicare and Medicaid and also expanded Social Security benefits for retirees, widows, the disabled and college-aged students, financed by an increase in the payroll tax cap and rates.

- **The Food Stamp Act of 1964**, which made the food stamps program a permanent addition to the increase in poverty.

- **The Economic Opportunity Act of 1964.** This thing established the Job Corps, the VISTA program, the federal work-study program and a number of other initiatives. All failed, but no one even tried to fix them.

- **The Head Start Program of 1965**- This was another 1965 fiasco, but no one seemed to address it that way and poverty continued to skyrocket and more and more money was being paid to non-workers.

- **The Elementary and Secondary Education Act**, signed into law in 1965, subsidizing school districts with a large share of impoverished students. This stupid thing has been changed to something called *"No Child Left Behind Act"*. This actually should be called ALL CHILDREN LEFT BEHIND as passing school classes now does not require learning so the poor stay poor.

Food Stamps-The sad facts are that by 2012, 4 million Americans were not consider poor because they were paid food stamps as shown below which now costs our country almost $50 billion a year and rising at an unbelievable, out of control rate. The $50Billion could be used to give the people jobs and get them out of slavery.

126

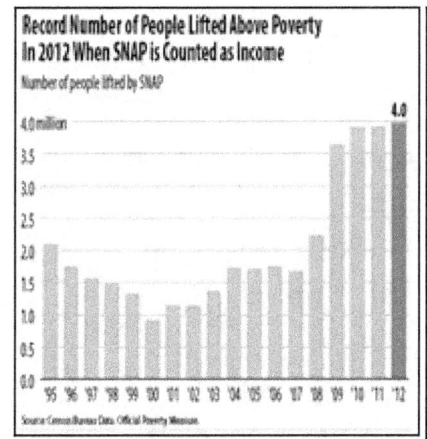

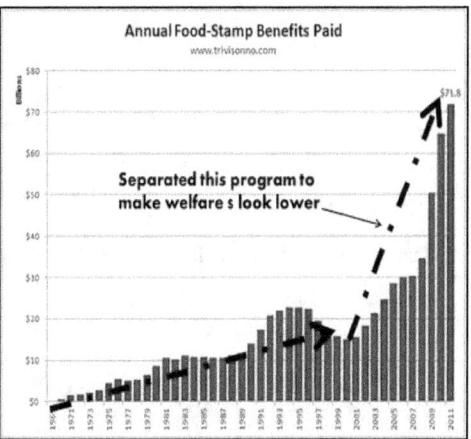

The second chart above simply shows that the Federal government tried to hide the huge expansion of "welfare" payments in 2000 by separating and expanding the Food Stamp or SNAP provision. As it skyrocketed, government officials were saying they were reducing the poverty slave money handouts.

Here is a sad fact. According to government surveys, the typical family that is identified as poor has air conditioning, cable or satellite TV, and a computer in his home. Forty percent have a wide screen HDTV and another 40 percent have internet access. Three quarters of the poor own a car and roughly a third have two or more cars.

These are not the statistics of poor people they are the statistics of poverty slaves made by an out of control government.

Poverty Rise-According to OPM [official poverty measures], overall poverty rates increased from only 14 percent in 1967 to 15 percent in 2012 which is totally horrible, is not even near the truth as so much money is being pumped into the poor to make it look like they are not poor it just makes you sick. The supplemental data eliminating the artificial offsets show the poverty rates are nearly double [18% to 33%].

- **Slavery making Earned income Credits** alone made it appear that 6.7 million people were not in what has been called the poverty level or 5%.
- **Slavery making Child Tax Credit** is said to have artificially reduce poverty level numbers by something like 10%.
- **Slavery making expanded Social Security**
- **Slavery making Food Stamps** reduced poverty numbers by 4%
- **Slavery making housing subsidies** also have contributed to this fake anti-poverty push.

The chart below shows the official poverty rate, the explosion of government enslavement money being pushed and the poverty increase minus this massive fake money that forces people into the enslavement of poverty.

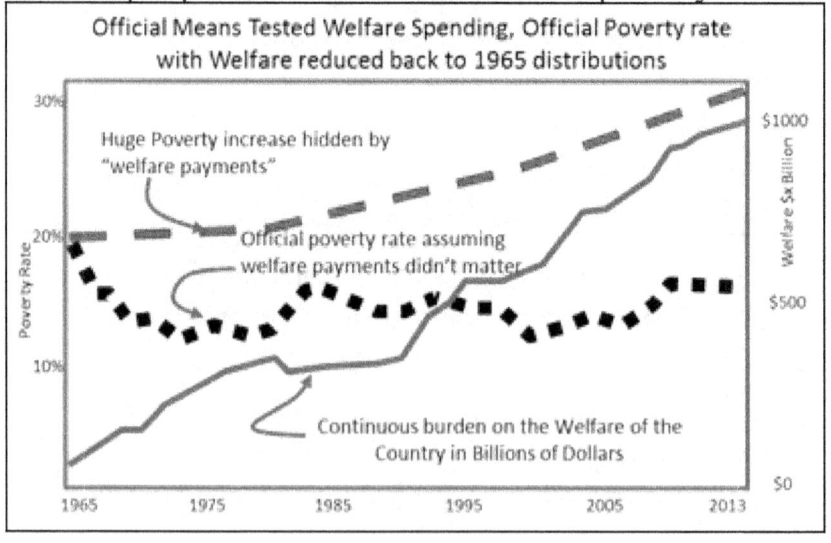

Slow the Welfare Spiral of Death

We must also reduce population of continuation. I am sorry to say, some people who cannot provide for themselves have offspring that they cannot provide for. There has to be a way to halt this spiral. One possibility is that welfare payments or subsistence must have a price. While having a child on subsistence should always be allowed, it seems only practical that a second child should not be permitted. If someone tries to continue, all payments SHOULD be removed. One thing that is apparent. If a mother can have a child and she is able to take on that effort, she certainly could be working.

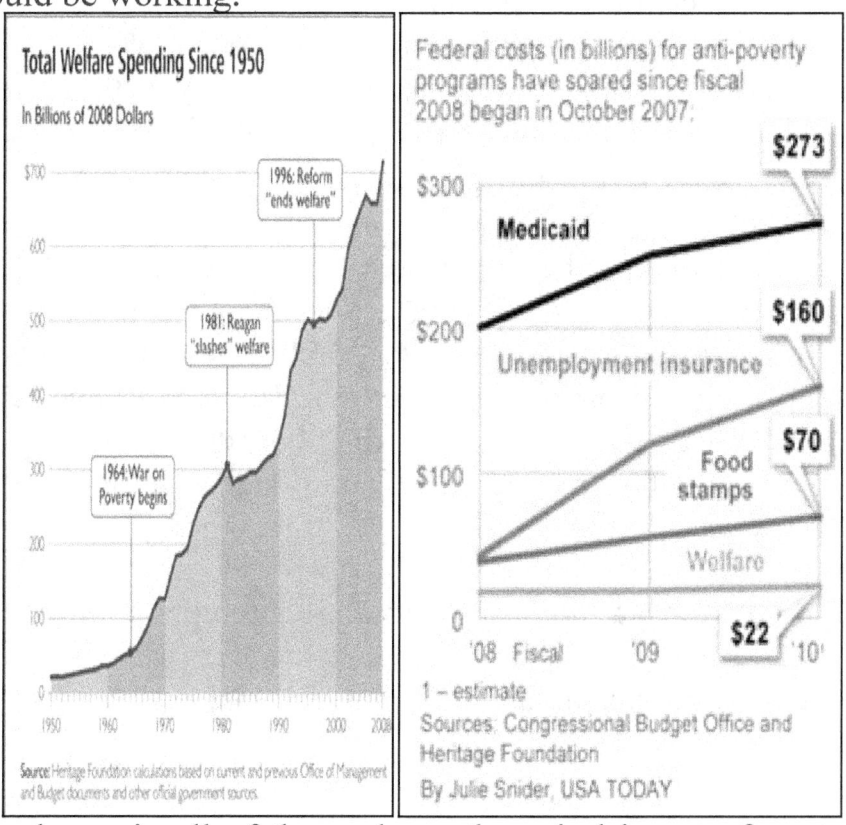

As shown in all of these charts the spiral is out of control. All the time, we can see from the last chart that4 the federal government says they only provide $22 Billion for welfare and it remains constant while food stamps, extended unemployment dollars, and Medicaid all skyrocket to keep the welfare cost seeming to stay constant.

What things HAVE to be done?

Everything must go and immediately be spent to get people to work or we are done for.

- Quit providing daycare for free, have poverty slaves work as daycare personnel.
- Don't extend unemployment; provide interim jobs for people while they are looking. Spend money getting them a job. Incentivize industry with money usually spent force individuals to not work.
- Reduce food programs to subsistence with equal pressure to help get those needing job the jobs they need.
- Pay money to industry to train the low wage earners rather than trying t5o give low wage earners money on the side.
- Eliminate earned income credit immediately. The least you should ever pay to your government is zero.
- Eliminate the national medical and tuition elements and fix the greed problem other ways. If anyone believes it will cost less to go to the hospital because the government is paying them additional money is super crazy.

Building a strong moral direction and attempts to eliminate poverty slavery will help, but we need to also Control Workforce Expansion and enhance National pride and at the same time.

Control Workforce Expansion

A country is built on resources. In America a vast amount of natural resources are coupled with the ingenuity and drive associated with something we can call the <u>blessings of Liberty we give to ourselves and our posterity.</u> We saw this special something during World War II especially as our country united and we became the absolute masters of the world for a time. In a different way, the same resource of liberty minded colonists was responsible for some of the outcome that would initially build our Country. I know a lot of the victory stemmed from the short-sided vision of the British, but for many, the beginnings of our nation was a do or die consideration brought on by a national fervor and pride. Both of these factors, natural resources and the lust for liberty, work together, only when growth of both are combined and in unison. If natural resources are too quickly diminished, the country is lost. If the population loses its patriotic population and desire for freedom, the country is lost. One of the most devastating ways to lose patriotic populations is by elimination of jobs. Our founders and subsequent lawmakers established a reasonable way to reduce the devastation of loss of jobs.

This was by restriction in population growth. As the nation expanded, entry of immigrants allowed for expansion of jobs. As the growth subsided, restriction was not only desirable, it was of immeasurable need. We could not take away the livelihood of Americans and survive.

Today, everything is all out of control. We must remove the huge numbers of illegal aliens in our country. I know some have told you these people were immigrants, but that simply is not so. A country has a specific limit to resources including jobs, land, civilization, structures for commerce, food, etc. and <u>we must regulate how fast or slow our country expands</u> so that the opportunity for freedoms exist in our country. It has been successfully accomplished 2 times in the 20th century and if it is not done again, we will soon lose our rightful place in the world. We will soon lose the capability to provide for the General Welfare. We will soon be in a death spiral.

Promote the General Welfare

Just what does it mean to promote the General Welfare anyway? Our federal Government does some of this. Certainly, there is general protection of the land and assurance of some reasonable existence, but the ones that have been in the news lately are in three parts; protection of our livelihood, protection from internal and external enemies, and protection from greed. There are many issues that are touched by this one term, but one that is most misunderstood is the capture and deportation of harmful illegal aliens that I previously mentioned. Only a couple of brave Presidents in the last 80 years have done their duty to the Constitution and to America in this regard. I know deportation sounds heartless and cruel to those outside the United States, but let me tell you something important. If the President and Congress keep doing nothing about this elimination of jobs, artificial reduction of wages, putting substantial pressures on monetary capabilities of our

132

government, and the unsupportable care of those who are not Americans, our own country will die.

Have you ever heard the ridiculous notion that if we removed illegal aliens in an effort to assure the common welfare of the Americans by reducing pressure on our job market jobs, reducing infiltration of those owing allegiance and patriotism to other countries, and limiting entrance of those who would instigate harm on Americans, would backfire?

- Some have said there is no harm in flooding our country with people without control as our joblessness and cost to support those entering skyrockets. I know you think these "migrants" are taking nasty jobs and helping our country, but this is all a lie as billions and billions are being provided to keep these people alive.

- Some have said there can be no issue with allowing uncontrolled millions aligned with countries outside our borders as they are just as patriotic as the next American, but that is a lie as American honored events are being forgotten and replaced by those that do not offend outsiders.

- Some have said Americans have too much and should allow those with less to infiltrate our borders at the cost of hardship to Americans because it makes those who don't lose their livelihoods feel better. This is a lie. There are no winners in this practice, not even the intruders.

- Many have said getting rid of these criminals from our workforce would be a failure as no one would take the menial jobs and America would suffer severely!! This is a lie. Once the anti-Constitution payments are reduced, people will work and begin winning back their freedom. Certainly you cannot make getting a job a punishment as the system is today.

I want you to think about this just a little as we find millions of high school and college kids unable to find work. Think about it as our reducing standard of living and welfare rolls are such that <u>over half of Americans</u> now are getting money and aid from our government [to survive] rather than having the resources to support it as John Kennedy told Americans was their duty. Think about it as America's Day was recently banned from a High School so that it would not "offend anyone". Think about it as wages are artificially driven downward as illegal workers stay quiet when their "Owners" pay them much less than Americans eliminating opportunity of Americans having those same jobs and the gestapo control of the farming industries and other task masters are loosed.

Deportation and Hoover

When we really have to, we deport all the illegal aliens and we are better for a while. Such is the case of Herbert Hoover's actions that assured <u>over a million illegal aliens were deported and tens of thousands work visa aliens "encouraged" to leave</u>. This operation would be known as "Operation Wetback" just like later operations but this one was in 1931. This President took what would today be considered a politically unpopular position by rounding up and deporting illegal aliens to create jobs for US Citizens. This first attempt occurred shortly after the banker-induced Stock Market Crash of 1929 when President Herbert Hoover ordered the round-up and deportation of illegals by the US Immigration and Naturalization Service. The Hoover roundup sent over **one million Mexican illegal**

aliens packing—freeing up jobs for out-of-work US citizens. In addition, some <u>47 thousand Mexican nationals who were in the country legally, with visas, also opted to leave</u> due to rising animosity by out-of-work Americans for any foreigner in the United States with a job. *Operation Wetback* was launched in the Southwest: Arizona, California, New Mexico and Texas. But deportees also came from Colorado, Illinois, Michigan, and New York. Since Mexican illegals tried hard to remain under the radar screen, few of them traveled far beyond the Border States, thus we can assume that most of the deportees from the States north of the Mason-Dixon Line were legal residents. During the Hoover years, <u>immigration to the United States was virtually stopped</u>. The Hoover deportations caused an outcry from the Mexican government demanding to know what gave Hoover the right to deny Mexican citizens the right to jobs in the United States under what was called the *"Good Neighbor Policy"* set in motion by Woodrow Wilson in 1913. Our President didn't care about his character being mashed in the ground; he worried about putting Americans back to work and increasing the General Welfare. He did what was needed. We can believe the effects were greatly appreciated by Americans, but in the depths of the Great Depression, details of the success are hard to read.

Roosevelt and Truman Opened the Floodgate

By the end of World War II, President Roosevelt had eliminated all the good from Hoover. During these days there were no jobs for US citizens. Unlike Hoover, Roosevelt had been in office to "help" the monster farming masters. Under Roosevelt's Public Law 78 <u>agricultural giants</u>, who needed dirt cheap labor, were allowed to import labor from Mexico even if all immigration quotas had been completely filled. Let me tell you how horrible this law was for the common welfare of Americans. Twenty five percent of the American labor force was still out of work and as much a 70% of the work force was out of work in the farm States while Roosevelt allowed illegals to be shipped in as fast as they could get them. As one would expect, Roosevelt's hands-off caused illegal alien immigration to increase by 6000%. America was in horrible condition and Truman came along.

By 1954, Truman was completely useless in this regard. The INS estimated that illegals were again crossing the US border at the rate of one million per year. The INS, as ordered by Harry Truman, went through the motions of rounding up illegal aliens and migrant workers who overstayed their visas. With his efforts against the powerful, Truman only was able to deport about 30 thousand Mexicans during his seven years in office. Then Eisenhower came along.

Eisenhower Saves Jobs

In keeping with his oath of office and the Constitution, Dwight D. Eisenhower and the Congress of the United States took on this delicate patriotic necessity and removed a very large portion of the illegal aliens. While we didn't have as severe an issue as we do today, it was estimated that 3-million had walked and waded northward over a period of several years with little interference from the previous President, Truman, for jobs in California, Arizona, Texas, and points beyond. It was a mess and people began losing their livelihoods. A Truman-initiated study on Mexican migratory labor in 1950 found that cotton growers in Texas paid migrant workers about half what a US citizen was paid to chop cotton. Eisenhower was stuck will cleaning up the mess created by the open door polices 73rd and 82nd

Congresses. As Eisenhower took office, <u>illegal immigrants were now crossing at the rate of about 3 million per year.</u> When Eisenhower assumed the Oval Office, illegal alien migration was one of his top priorities. President Eisenhower knew what the Constitution required him to do. He cut off this illegal traffic. He did it quickly and decisively with only 1,075 United States Border Patrol agents. This is less than one-tenth of today's force. The operation is still highly praised among veterans of the Border Patrol. Before Eisenhower became president, the *New York Times* reported on the issue of illegal infiltration. Here is a short excerpt "*The rise in illegal border-crossing by Mexican 'wetbacks' to <u>a current rate of **more** than 1,000,000 cases a year</u> has been accompanied by a curious relaxation in ethical standards extending all the way from the farmer-exploiters of this contraband labor to the highest levels of the Federal Government.*" Profits from illegal labor led to the kind of corruption that apparently worried Eisenhower more than most.

It is difficult to estimate the number of illegal aliens forced to leave by Eisenhower's operation in 1953. The INS claimed as many as 1,300,000, though the number officially apprehended was less than this total. The INS estimates concluded that many illegals feared apprehension by the government and voluntarily repatriated themselves before and during the operation. INS agents in the San Antonio district alone, which included most of Texas outside of El Paso, <u>saw an estimated 500,000 to 700,000 fleeing</u> to Mexico just as the campaign began. The whole thing took only 2 years leaving almost all illegals gone. Major opposition by Senators Lyndon B. Johnson (D) of Texas and Pat McCarran (D) of Nevada did not deter Ike as he eliminated the problem that was keeping jobs from

Americans. The result of Ike's Operation Wetback was stunning. Gen. Joseph by early 1954 was capturing illegal immigrants from Mexico. Beginning from the Rio Grande Valley, Wetback spread quickly; <u>illegal aliens were sent back by forced and armed military</u>. On the first day of Operation Wetback, about 5 thousand illegal aliens were "gone". From the day after, <u>about 1,100 illegal aliens were sent back per day</u>. The United States government had shown that they would not tolerate illegal activities that would reduce Constitutional general welfare of Americans. Let me show you a fairly simple chart concerning Eisenhower's efforts. It's called the Nonfinancial Corporation Labor share. What you seen in the chart is that Eisenhower's operation wetback <u>increased this labor factor by about 6%</u> from 1953 until 1955 and after a short recession it rebounded to about the same level until his Presidency had ended. Once the Kennedy/ Johnson reign started there was massive pressure on the job market 1966 that did not recover until about 1970 when Nixon took control of the United States. You may notice that since GW Bush became president and through the Obama reign this number has been steadily decreasing while money spent on welfare has been skyrocketing.

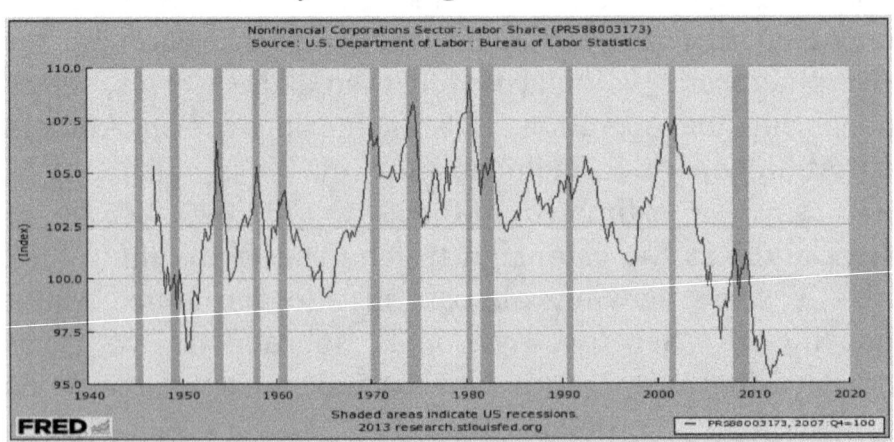

Let me show you one more chart. The following Chart from the Beareau of Labor Statistics data shows percentage of Americans working from 1950 until 1976 and the participation percentage of Americans in the work force averaging around 60%, but notice something important as we look at what happened after Eisenhower's elimination of Illegal's in 1954. People took the jobs left by the illegals in record numbers causing a huge jump the reduction of unemployed of Americans as you would expect. Don't let someone tell you Amercians will not take menial jobs. We can assume the same thing happened after the similar action taken by President Hoover, but that data is unavailable.

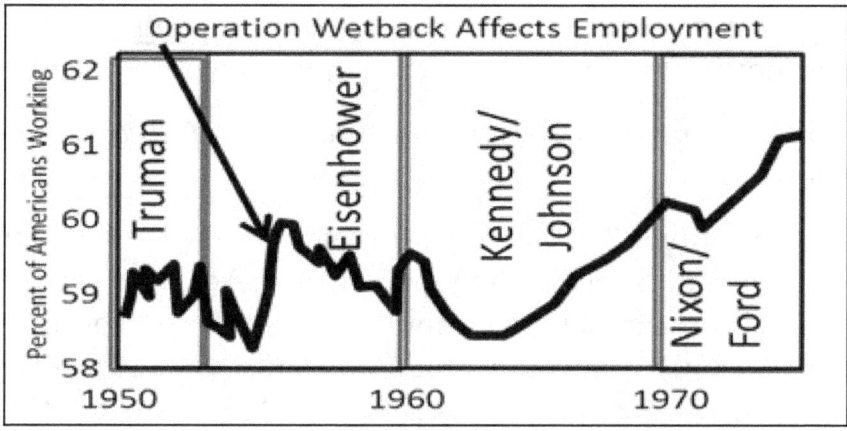

Since Eisenhower

We find failure after failure to protect Americans and assure reasonable welfare to Americans. Instead of discouraging and preventing illegals form assaulting our country, Presidents did the opposite and encourage, allowed, praised, and comforted . Presidents Reagan, Clinton, and Obama were some of the worst. While Reagan did say it was the worst thing he did, he still continued to allow Amwericans to lose jobs and to put great pressure on our social programs. President Obama has no such regret.

President Obama's Horror -Last but not least, this president ordered the entire justice function of our country to ignore all illegals and even help them come into our country. Millions have entered and the rate is expanding under his watch as his quasi-amnesty of ignoring has done its worst.

An amnesty is a reward to those breaking the law. Issuing an amnesty to illegal aliens only encourages more illegal immigration into the United States.

After the 1986 amnesty, illegal immigration increased significantly. Census Bureau 2000 data indicate that 700,000 to 800,000 illegal aliens settle in the U.S. each year, with somewhere between 12 and **40 million** illegal aliens now currently living in the United States.

Amnesty benefits neither our society nor those being amnestied.

The only thing you can be assured of with this huge population of illegal aliens is crime. According to the Immigration and Naturalization Service, the average illegal alien had only a seventh grade education and earned less than $9,000 a year [EVEN IF HE HAD BEEN AMNESTIED] The only difference is that it was easier for them to get additional welfare.

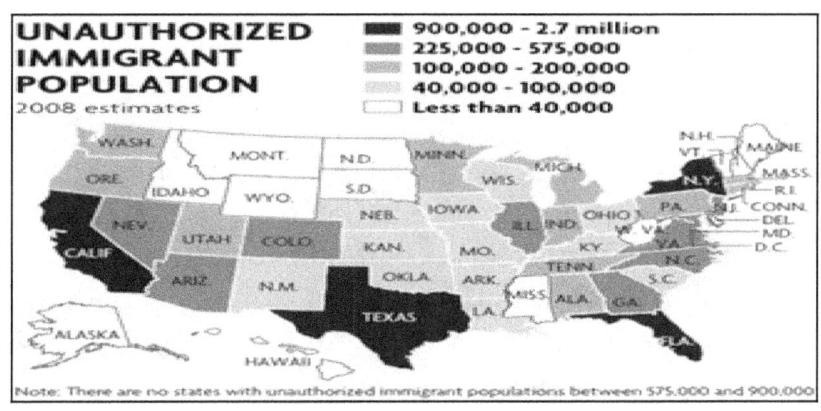

UNAUTHORIZED IMMIGRANT POPULATION
2008 estimates

- 900,000 - 2.7 million
- 225,000 - 575,000
- 100,000 - 200,000
- 40,000 - 100,000
- Less than 40,000

Note: There are no states with unauthorized immigrant populations between 575,000 and 900,000

As the preceding map shows, in 2008 there were **over 2 million illegal aliens living in Florida, in Texas, in California, and in New York**. Besides those there were 9 States with about ½ million each and another 21 have about 100 thousand or more. These numbers have risen significantly, but a general map shows concentration of those reducing our General Welfare.

STATE COSTS OF ILLEGAL IMMIGRATION
American taxpayers spend over **$84 billion** dollars annually to subsidize illegal immigration.

FAIR
FEDERATION FOR AMERICAN IMMIGRATION REFORM
www.FAIRUS.org

While no one should use the term immigration when discussing illegal criminals, the following chart shows the estimated costs to each state because of these unregistered aliens who should not be here. The chart comes from the Federation for Immigration Reform who found that $84 Billion has been spent by taxpayers each year to subsidize these intruders. A lot of people could be put back to work for $84 billion every year. Additionally it should be noted that the federal government just put out an indication that the Affordable Healthcare Act now is costing about ¾ billion dollars to support illegal medicine.

Things that we should worry about.

- There is no question that removing the Illegals will reduce joblessness.

- There is no question it will make our country safer.

- There is no question that removing all the illegals has been done 2 times before so there is NO Consititutional issue no matter what anyone says.

- In many ways it is political suicide to do what Eisenhower and Hoover did, but that does not mean it shouldn't be done.

- There is no question that the $84 billion a year spent protecting the Illegal aliens would go a long way at making all Americans more comfortable by creating a huge number of jobs.

While removing illegals may mean separating families for a time, we must increase to concept of family even if it means converting some of the illegal aliens to resident status. If we don't find ways to strengthen families, we are doomed.

Bring Back Families

The bond associate with family helps secure stability needed to build a nation. Without this stability, no lasting position in society can be sustained, no push toward accomplishment, no direction away from perversion, nor restriction of attitude to allow united interface of people. The separation of family is amplified by current slavery methods. If a man claims his family, taxes are increase, welfare payments are decrease or eliminated, and fathers are removed from the lives of their children. We must eliminate this issue. Certainly the work for money method will help, but there should not be a penalty for being married, in fact, a woman should always be required to identify the father and no funding for support should be established until AFTER the father is contacted and support is established in some way. The payment for work instead of free money and services will help here as well. More people will stay together and with more fathers heading families, crime will be reduced.

Indeed, one of the biggest accomplishments of the War on Poverty seems to have been the proliferation of single parent households and children being born out of wedlock, but the creation of poverty slaves is right up there with it. . In 1964 the percentage of American children born to unwed mothers was approximately 4%. Today the figure has skyrockets to 800% of that number. According to studies by HHS and others, that's largely because the welfare state has made such a choice not only feasible but preferable. Here is what they said.

> *Holding constant a wide range of variables, including income, education, and urban vs. suburban setting, the study found that a 50 percent increase in the value of AFDC and food-stamp payments led to a 43 percent increase in the number of out-of-wedlock births.*

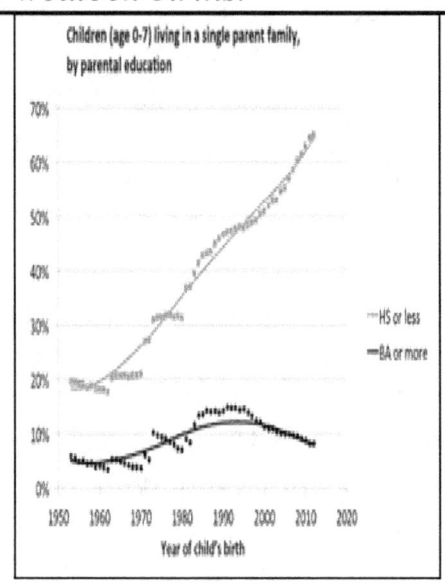

One thing noted as the family unit is destroyed is that more and more people are ending up in prison.

Stronger Families Reduce Crime

Certainly another accomplishment of the War on poverty has been incarcerations. This issue and the next on are getting more and more closely aligned as more and more of the arrests today are for drug use or sales. The statistics are staggering. The next graph shows incarcerations from 1925 until 2008 and what we see is that they stayed about the same until about 1970 then everything is sky rocking. The last chart shows that the United States has 20 times as many in prisons as most other countries so we must understand our nation is sick. One thing that will help fgr3atly is to slow the use of drugs.

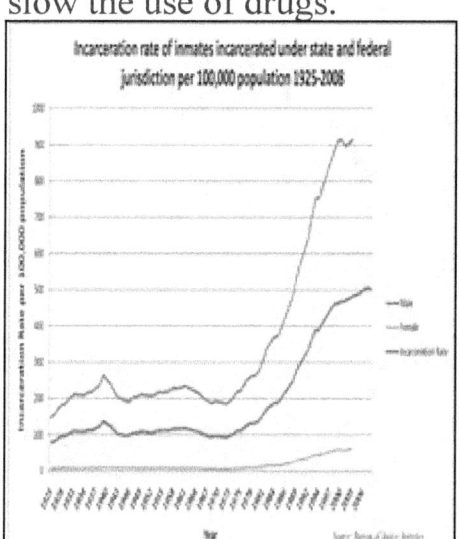
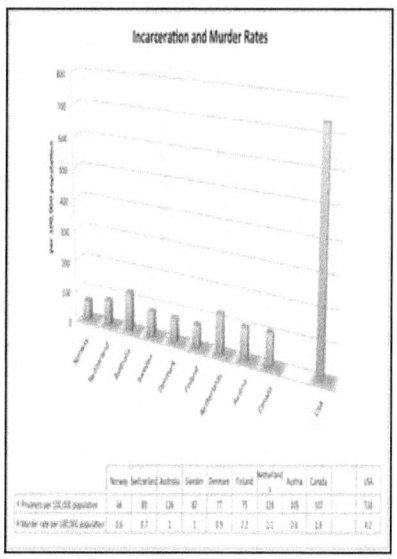

 One thing noticed as family ties get stronger is that baby killing will go down.

Don't Glorify Baby Killing

Some Americans try to say killing babies is the right of the mother and I'm not really getting into that but to say sometimes killing a baby helps the welfare of a woman, but it almost never helps the baby. This custom does not enhance the family union or strength of a family at all. Many use a religious conviction to show concern for this glorified abortion concept we have called Planned parenthood, but what we find is that the institute simply is a bucket to pour federal money into so that less will be available to support the needy.

The following chart shows that every year the finding for this thing has gone up and up until 2011.

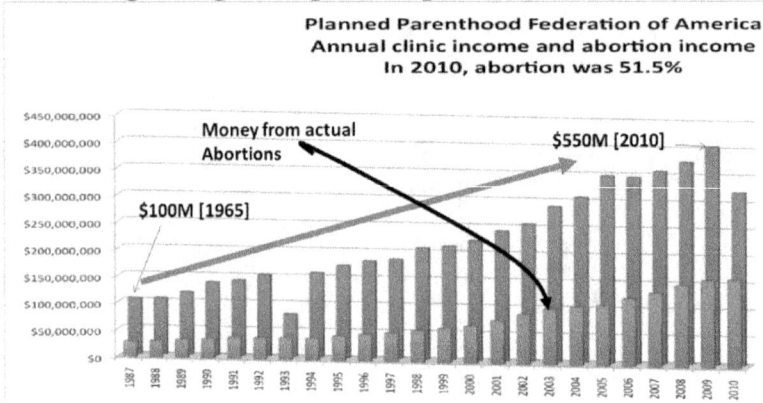

Planned Parenthood Federation of America
Annual clinic income and abortion income
In 2010, abortion was 51.5%

Interestingly enough, the people running this thing are getting super rich and think we should keep things the way they are. The next list shows many "executives" are making up to $½ million or more. Isn't it appropriate to call them execute----ites?

PPFA Top Corporate Employee Salaries

President	Cecile Richards	$590,928
Chief Financial Officer	Wallace D'Souza	$257,603
Chief Operations Officer	Lisa David	$419,028
Chief development Officer	Sandra Sedacca	$391,802
Chief Information Officer	Thomas Subak	$307,484
Chief Experience Officer	Dawn Laguens	$481,126
SR VP & General Council	Debra Alligood White	$324,098
Managing Director of Development	Jennie Thompson	$318,283
VP PP Experience	Molly Eagan	$294,927
Nat'l Director Principal & major gifts	Elizabeth Liley	$263,335
SR Principle gifts officer	Ann McGuiness	$247,835
VP HIT & business initiatives	Eileen Twiggs	$247,606

To show how very useful this has been for our country. The next chart shows the number of babies having abortions.

	THE ALARMING TALLY						
	Abortions carried out on under 16s						
Year	Ten or under	11	12	13	14	15	Total under 16
2002	0	1	14	153	907	2,658	3,733
2003	0	0	10	138	1,023	2,796	3,967
2004	0	0	15	142	877	2,722	3,756
2005	0	1	7	129	946	2,703	3,786
2006	0	0	5	130	907	2,948	3,990
2007	0	0	11	152	1,008	3,205	4,376
2008	0	1	6	159	931	3,016	4,113
2009	0	0	4	132	911	2,776	3,823
2010	0	0	2	134	906	2,676	3,718
TOTAL	0	3	74	1,269	8,416	25,500	35,262

Notice we have about the same every year from 2002 until 2010 as they try to glamorize abortion. I'm not saying they cause babies to get pregnant, but they are not fixing anything. The next 2 charts show that abortion numbers have risen between 1972 and 2010, but something has recently changed that may help. A republican congress enacted ove 200 restrictions on this organization that may slow our demise.

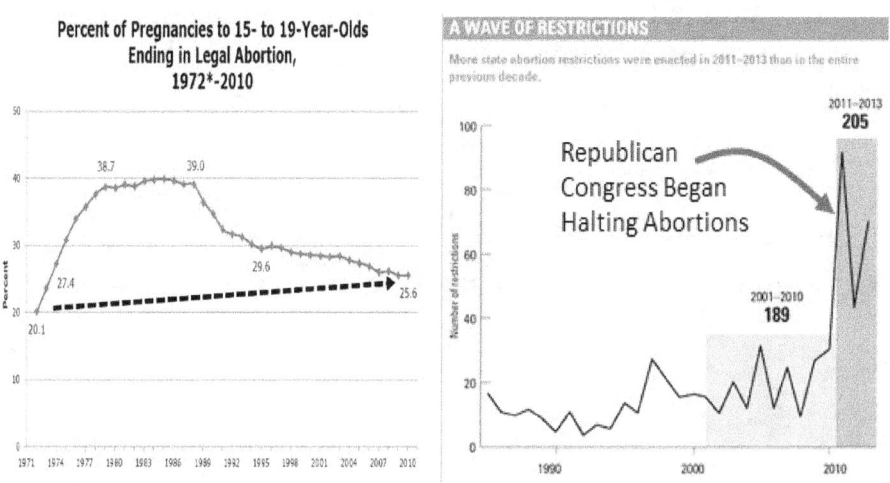

I think I had better bring up the 2nd amendment for completeness as there are spectacular errors in reporting.

Second Amendment

A well-regulated Militia, being necessary to the security of a Free State, the right of the people to keep and bear Arms, shall not be infringed.

The idea of <u>bearing</u> rather than <u>having</u> is an interesting issue. It would seem that if you are allowed to "bear" arms against the State as implied by the Militia statement, there MUST be an allowance to HAVE THOSE ARMS---JUST IN CASE.

Today this is being turned into a joke. People have banners against having the ability to own and use weapons as something nasty, but this was specifically introduced to assure the federal government would not get too controlling as was witnessed in all other societies around the world. If the government becomes oppressive, people should have the right to protect their family from that oppression. Some have indicated guns are making us a dangerous country, but let's look at the facts. In the UN survey from 2000 USA had 5 homicides per 100,000 people.

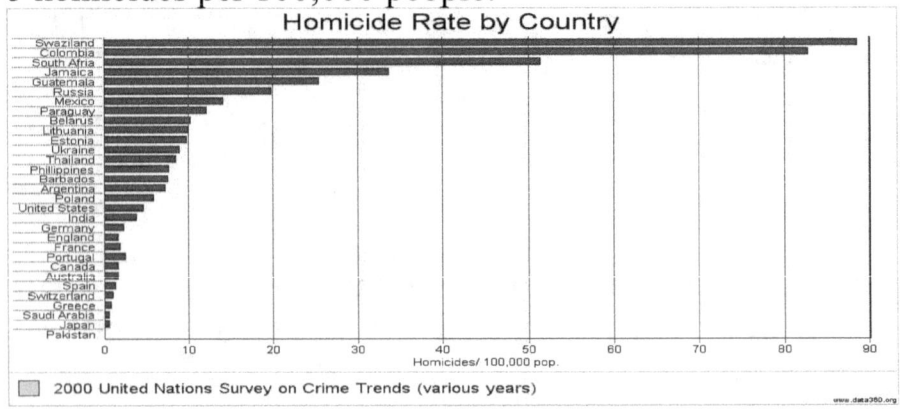

2000 United Nations Survey on Crime Trends (various years)

As we move to 2004, the United States was so low it didn't even make the list as shown next. Additionally we see that violent crimes are reducing just about every year. [See below right]

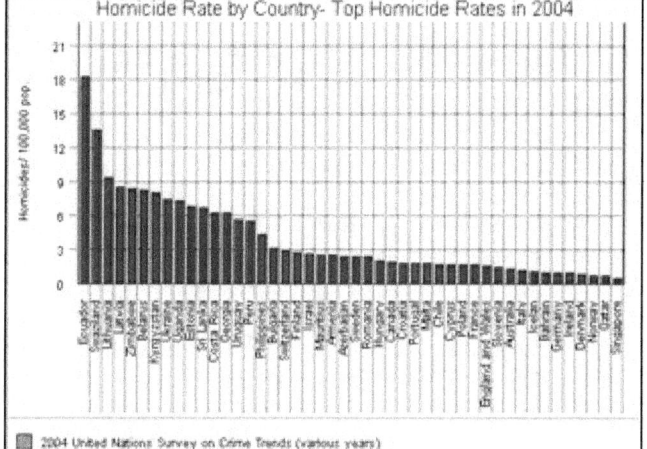

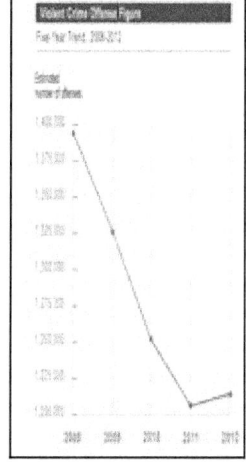

So what is happening? The next 2 charts tell the story as people can protect themselves. Today USA has twice the number of guns per person that all of the countries listed in the chart next left and since 2000 there has been a steady rise in the number of new gun owners protecting themselves.

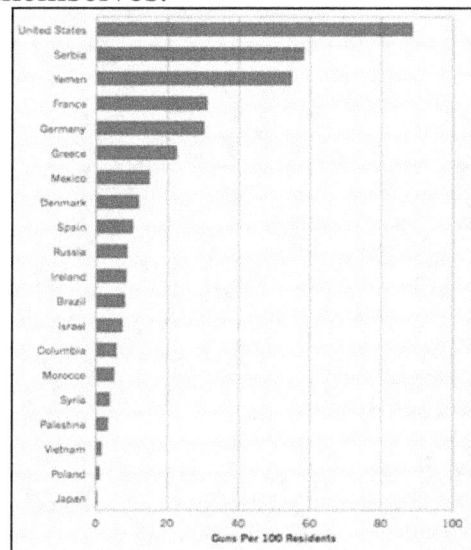

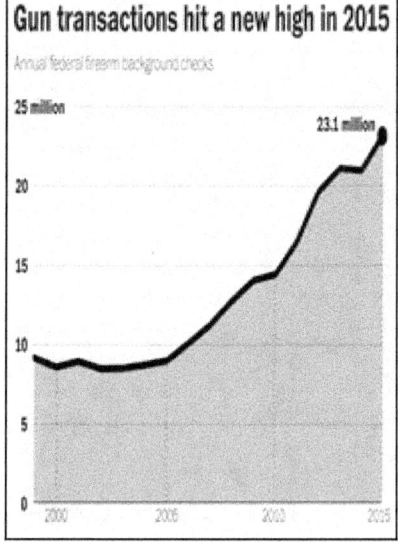

There are less killings because hoodlums don't want to be shot. I know everywhere you look someone is saying the United States is dangerous because of guns, but this is simply not what the data says.

We also need to understand what the word DISPARAGE means in the ninth amendment before it is too late.

Understand the Ninth Amendment

While this one is popular today and its meaning has been used to give the Federal Government more and more power, it is time to replace this bad law for something that will make us great again. Here is what it says.

The enumeration in the Constitution <u>of certain rights</u> shall not be construed to deny or disparage others retained by the people.

Initially you just think it is nonsensical. If someone feels they have the right to kill someone, but the Constitution says you should not do it, we should not disparage his right to feel that way. Some have twisted this one around to say anything not explicitly identified in the Constitution is a right retained by an individual. This in no way says this, but our Federal Courts have used these words for a long time now to take rights away from the majority. Here is their reasoning----If the Constitution doesn't specifically say starving a person until they die is bad, one can do that because it is the lack of food killing him not the person.

Recently this has been used as a way of forcing minority rule in our country. We cannot survive like that. Yes the 9th amendment says we cannot disparage [CERTAIN RIGHTS]

- Yes; it does sort of say Satanist and their ways simply because the majority hates it or are scared of it as it would disparage them. This interpretation is why putting up a Christmas tree at Christmas time is forced out.

- Yes; it does "sort of" say the Illegal Aliens should not be sent home simply because they broke our laws, caused great hardship on our available jobs and need government services we cannot afford to survive. This interpretation is killing America as recent numbers show that almost $Billion is being given to illegal aliens for the government sponsored healthcare that is strangling all Americans. When other services are added, it is obvious we cannot support the entire world.

- Yes; it does sort of say that a trans-sexual person must not be considered mentally challenged. Just because this illness was called gender dysphoria or gender identity disorder (GID) for years, we need to change and try to be more transsexual ourselves. We should let them have children to work on their little minds as well.

This was not the original intent of the Amendment, but now we need to reestablish what it is saying.

Only CERTAIN rights are *not be construed to deny or disparage others. Let's list the main ones.*

Our government shall not allow anyone to—
- *kill another*
- *steal from another person*
- *kidnap another or hold him against his will*
- *Harm another without cause.*

Certainly the last one is the trickier one. Should the government allow someone to harm a bigamist, or a fat person, or a stupid person, or an ugly person? The question gets a little more problematic are we cannot understand what "harm" means. While there are issues concerning establishing harm, this amendment cannot be used to stifle the reasonable lifestyle of the majority. It never was intended for that.

So far you can see we are getting closer to the Utopian Communist State. Everyone is cared for; as someone gets sick he is treated; all children get through school and many stay high on drugs so they can't see any badness in the world, but can anyone have freedom in a communist environment?

Can We have Communism and Freedom?

Some claim we can have Free Communism. Just listen to the news. They even hide the things that sound bad to paint a beautiful picture as we slide into blind comfort. We can't allow those who don't work to meet a limited level of existence simply because it seems like the right thing to do and ignore what happens to our country. Most of these people have gone out to see if there is work, but found none so they did their part. As I stated before, today over 50% of the Americans are compensated for not working in some way. Many of those make their entire livelihood by government handouts. Some have to claim that the downward spiral of government handout living has been going on for generations in their family. With half the population voting to either get governmental money or starving with no job opportunity, the cycle is assured to continue until the end of a society. First will be the transition into a formal communist government which is followed by vast levels of poverty or a trumped up monetary system until it all falls apart. Greece is beginning to see the end but still hold onto unreasonable government pensions without anything to provide the funds. Rome died that way and most other societies lost their freedom slowly. Some of those holding to the rich rewards of passive hand-outliving believe they will be dead before the end comes so there is no downside. The problem is we have children.

Limits of General Welfare-We are going to try to understand the limits of General Welfare, what it means, how it can be enacted and how we can begin change the mindset and start to be responsible, patriotic, citizens doing "for our country". Some say it is simply too late, but there is a seed of freedom in Americans that cannot be broken. We can develop the seed and spring a new unified country if we take the hard steps.

Steps to Freedom

Here are some of the steps needed. You won't like them all and you may even fell sick to your stomach with some, but our country is festering, and spiraling into a death which will be far worst to all. The answer to the original question is we cannot have communism and Freedom. Simply calling it socialism doesn't help either.

- *We Must Control Workforce Expansion*
- *We Must Establish Jobs not Slavery*
- *We Must Eliminate Glamorized Poverty*
- *We Must Slow the Welfare Spiral*
- *We must teach our children about how to work for liberty, not freedom from work driving them to slavery*
- *We must not punish the majority by coddling deviates, militants, and the godless and refocus in a moral direction.*
- *We must support marriage, not punish it*
- *We must bring pride in America back by focusing on helping the majority rather than killing the middle class.*

By doing these steps, our country has a chance. Without doing something different, we are doomed no matter how well someone wrote a Constitution. Unfortunately that will not be enough as our country has also been overrun by uncontrolled greed, monopolistic industry, and a government that is bought by the powerful.

- *We must limit the control by the Federal Government over the States*
- *We Must Reduce the Stronghold of Monopolies*
- *We Must Establish More Control over Greed*
- *We must limit Industrial influence in our government.*

To start with, we must reinstitute the tenth Amendment.

Loss of the Tenth Amendment

This is a simple amendment that has been twisted into knots. It goes like this.

*The powers not delegated to the United States by the Constitution, nor prohibited by it to the States, are reserved to the States respectively, **or to the people**.*

Some have claimed the *"or the people"* part is to be ignored as it is saying the MAJORITY OF THE PEOPLE RULE THIS NATION, not the deviants or minorities.

It is also saying that States have EVERY power not given to the federal Government by Constitutional Authority this includes the following from Article 1 Section 8"
- To lay and collect Taxes
- To pay for the common Defense
- To pay for the General Welfare or our nation
- To borrow Money on the credit of the United States
- To regulate Commerce with foreign Nations
- To establish Rule of Naturalization and Bankruptcy
- To coin and regulate Money and punish counterfeiting
- To establish Post Offices
- To promote the Progress of Science and useful Arts
- To constitute Tribunals inferior to the Supreme Court
- To declare War, punish pirates, and repel invasion
- To raise and support an Army for no longer than two Years

- To provide and maintain a Navy
- To make Rules for land and naval Forces
- To execute the Laws of the Union
- To organize and train the Militia
- To make Laws for the above items <u>ONLY</u>
- To define and collect all Duties on Imports or Exports
- To determine and enter into any Agreement with a foreign Power

While there are many issues concerning overreach of our Federal Government, I'm going to just address 2 here. The first is the unconstitutional takeover of land by the Federal Government which has led to inequality of States and the Character of the tiny New England Statettes which has led to the inequality of States as well.

What About Controlling Federal Land?

Our Federal Government can only OWN land in accordance with 3 separate elements of the Constitution. While before the 10th Amendment, one might wonder about those areas no defined, but now we know those powers go to the States.

1. *The Federal Government can control less than **10 square miles** of State lands [if the State allows] for Enclaves [Forts and other needful Buildings].* They knew that an overseeing federal government must not gain too much control or the fabric of democratic republicanism will be shattered.
2. *The Federal Government can control all territories not yet established as States. Once they are States they have all rights of States.* This was placed in the Constitution to allow our country to pay debts by selling territorial land quickly to pay the Army, Navy, and war debt. It

was never to take land from States as it could limit State equality.

3. *The Federal Government can own property for enumerated purposes in accordance to the following: The Congress shall have power to dispose of and make all needful Rules and Regulations respecting the Territory or other Property belonging to the United States; and nothing in this Constitution shall be so construed as to Prejudice any Claims of the United States, or of any particular State.* If a State decides it does not want the Federal Government to control land inside their borders, they need only lay claim--- except for the 10 square miles thing.]

Today is we look at the worst breaches of the federal Government overreach here we see the tiny list below showing how much of the entire States are OWNED by the Federal Government illegally. Every year this travesty gets worse and worse.

Arizona	45%	New Mexico	35%
California	45%	Oregon	52%
Colorado	36%	Utah	66%
Idaho	64%	Washington	30%
Montana	30%	Wyoming	50%
Nevada	87%	Alaska	70%

Here is what we know. The federal government was not created to be the owner of the land; it was created expressly to get the "right of soil" out of the hands of a king – that is, out of the hands of government. The sovereign right of the king to own, to tax and control the use of land led directly to the Declaration of Independence in 1776, in the Treaty of Paris in 1783 was between the king of England and each of the enumerated states. Here is what the Treaty said specifically recognizes these states:

> *...to be free sovereign and <u>independent states</u>, that the king treats with them as such, and for himself, his heirs, and successors, relinquishes all claims to the government, propriety, and territorial rights of the same and every part thereof.*

While this doesn't have much to do with Constitutional law, it does show the States had the original power and simply provided a small amount to allow for their combined protection. That being said there was an attempt to make all States have similar power. [One might think of this by saying they wanted all States to control identical percentages of their own State land.]

What About State Equality

Let's look at this a minute by first reviewing Article IV, Section 3, Clause 1, which states: *New States may be admitted by the Congress into this Union; but no new State shall be formed or erected within the Jurisdiction of any other State; nor any State be formed by the Junction of two or more States, or Parts of States, without the Consent of the Legislatures of the States concerned as well as of the Congress.*

This has been known as the **Equal footing doctrine**, or **equality of the states.** The general court interpretation is this. *All states admitted to the Union under the Constitution since 1789 will enter on equal footing with the 13 states already in the Union at that time.*

Because of this Beginning with the admission of Tennessee in 1796, Congress has included in each state's act of admission a clause providing that it enters the Union "*on an equal footing with the original States in all respects whatever".*

Are all States on an Equal Footing?

This *"Equal Footing Doctrine,"* supposedly insured that all States were equal in their sovereign power. Article I, Section 8 specified how the federal government might acquire land and the purposes for which it could be acquired from the States [not in excess of 10 square miles for forts and similar buildings]. The 10th Amendment further declared that powers not explicitly granted to the federal government were retained by the states and the people. While no State has only given up 10 square miles Rhode Island has given about 16 square miles of space to the federal government 12 States have had to give up well over 16 thousand square miles. Some suggest, rightfully so, this is not Equal footing anymore. Below is a list of the various Federal land takeaways. Notice that the earlier States had the least taken away. Let's compare the new States to the old one.

States by least stolen land	Federal Acres [xM]	State Acres [xM]	Total %	States by least stolen land	Federal Acres [xM]	State Acres [xM]	Total %
Connecticut	0.01	3.1	0.3%	Wisconsin	1.79	35	5.1%
Iowa	0.11	35.9	0.3%	S. Dakota	2.64	48.9	5.4%
New York	0.09	30.7	0.3%	Minnesota	3.48	51.2	6.8%
Kansas	0.26	52.5	0.5%	West Virginia	1.14	15.4	7.4%
Rhode Island	0.01	0.68	0.8%	N. Carolina	2.42	31.4	7.7%
Illinois	0.39	35.8	1.1%	Vermont	0.46	5.9	7.8%
Maine	0.22	19.8	1.1%	Arkansas	3.16	33.6	9.4%
Nebraska	0.54	49	1.1%	Virginia	2.52	25.5	9.9%
Massachusetts	0.06	5	1.2%	Michigan	3.65	36.5	10.0%
Ohio	0.31	26.2	1.2%	Florida	4.58	34.7	13.2%
Oklahoma	0.71	44.1	1.6%	N. H.	0.80	5.8	13.8%
Indiana	0.39	23.2	1.7%	Hawaii	0.82	4.1	20.0%
Texas	3.03	168.2	1.8%	D.C.	0.01	0.04	21.0%
Pennsylvania	0.60	28.8	2.1%	Washington	12.17	42.7	28.5%
Delaware	0.03	1.3	2.4%	Montana	27.06	93.3	29.0%
Alabama	0.85	32.7	2.6%	New Mexico	27.00	77.8	34.7%
Maryland	0.20	6.3	3.1%	Colorado	23.87	66.5	35.9%
Missouri	1.64	44.2	3.7%	Arizona	28.06	72.7	38.6%
New Jersey	0.18	4.8	3.7%	California	45.89	100.2	45.8%
North Dakota	1.74	44.5	3.9%	Wyoming	29.97	62.3	48.1%
Georgia	1.49	37.3	4.0%	Oregon	32.59	61.6	52.9%
Kentucky	1.10	25.5	4.3%	Alaska	223.69	365.5	61.2%
South Carolina	0.85	19.4	4.4%	Idaho	32.59	52.9	61.6%
Louisiana	1.33	28.9	4.6%	Utah	34.20	52.7	64.9%
Tennessee	1.28	26.7	4.8%	Nevada	59.60	70.2	84.9%
Mississippi	1.54	30.2	5.1%	Total USA	622.31	2271	27.4%

161

This is getting worse every year as more and more unequal intrusion into various States shows our country is falling apart. To show this more reasonably, I split the United States in half If you live on the left side, the Federal Government takes away your land, but leaves the east coast alone almost always.

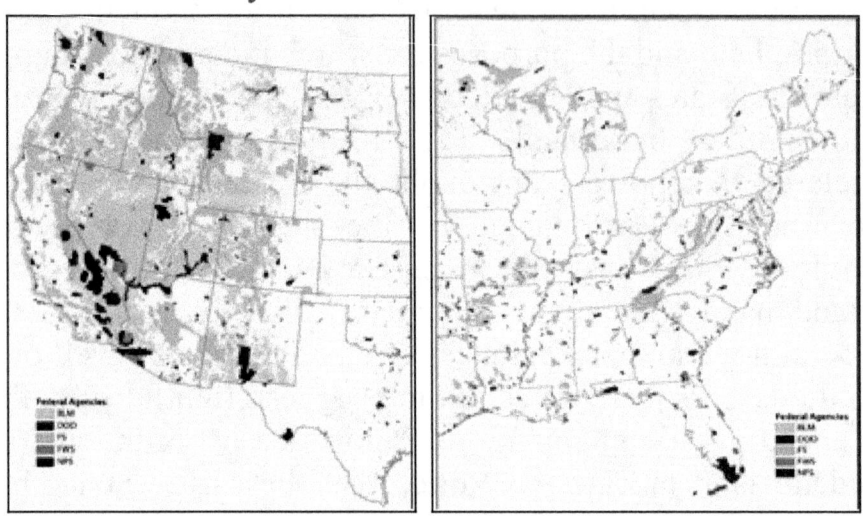

When Did the Federal Government Take State Powers?

When looking for the start to the major takeover of the federal government we find the New Deal days in the 1930s, but the driver for the major takeaway of our rights and privileges today are generally focus on the Federal Energy Regulatory Commission and in particular issues arising in control of energy. The court is well aware that the states had sovereign authority before the Union was ever formed in the 1790s. They assumed that status after the break with England in 1776, and they retained a good deal of that sovereignty under the Constitution – and, indeed, saw it explicitly safeguarded by the Tenth Amendment – usually thought of as the "states' rights" amendment. While it is mostly bad, there are some good signs.

Supreme Court and Federal Overreach

1819- Forced Central Bank-The court upheld the right of Congress to create a Bank of the United States, ruling that it was a <u>power implied</u> but not enumerated by the Constitution.

1824- Forced Federal Commerce Control-The court defined broadly Congress's <u>implied right</u> to regulate commerce.

1857-*Dred Scott* – The Court <u>defined the implied less human nature</u> of black people and that Congress had no right to ban slavery from U.S. territories.

2015-Government Overreach in Power Plants-"The Clean Power plan raises serious federalism concerns. It is well-established that it is incumbent upon the federal courts to be certain of Congress' intent before finding that federal law overrides the usual constitutional balance of federal and state powers....The states' authority over the intrastate generation and consumption of energy is one of the most important functions traditionally associated with the police powers of the states....EPA's interpretation of [the Clean Air Act] intrudes on that traditional state authority. By arrogating to itself the authority to choose favored and disfavored industries in the domestic energy field, EPA undermines the states' authority to independently assess the intrastate need for new power facilities, their economic feasibility, and rates and services." – *Excerpt from a legal filing in the Supreme Court on January 26 by 29 states urging the Justices to block the Obama administration's new Clean Power Plan that seeks to divert energy generation from plants fueled by coal and oil to plants powered by wind or solar, which EPA believes will benefit* *the environment by sharply reducing emissions of carbon dioxide.*

2015- luckily there has been a delay in this travesty- President Barack Obama received a strong rebuke from the Supreme Court for his attempt to make appointments when Congress was still technically in session.

2015 -*National Labor Relations Board vs. Noel Canning* came just as Speaker John Boehner announced plans to sue President Obama for executive overreach.

Statettes Versus States

Generally the Supreme Court has aided in the takeover of power by the federal Government. Certainly it is noticeable as more and more land is being taken over by the federal government to eliminate State Equality, but this equality thing was challenged early on. As I stated earlier, the tiny Statettes of New England caused most of the Civil Wars in our country simply because the tiny states had more representation that the massive ones. Why weren't the later States split apart to similar sizes of the New England Statettes? If we want to look at a beginning of this horrible downfall, there are many dates that could be used. I am only using the 1860s because the abuses were so hidden that most have no recollection of them and our nation was almost destroyed. If we can figure out how we survived then, it may help us today. While the 4th Civil War that occurred at this time didn't help, I'm talking about the destruction by government sponsored, government funded, and industrialization of monopolized commodities. The commodities were under-control for a time, but then Railroadians, Steel Manufacturers, Land speculators, Gold manipulators and others. If you went against the 'Puppet"

Presidents of this time, you could find yourself in a hidden prison. The first was named Abraham Lincoln, but Ulysses Grant was just as bad. Lincoln passed the Morrill Tariff on March 2, 1861. This immediately raised the effective <u>taxes on agrarian State products to **38%**</u> and greatly expanded the list of covered items. The Agrarian States didn't secede so <u>he passed a second one.</u> This second one <u>increased tariffs on imported goods to about triple what it had been under Tyler's burdening tariffs</u>

You might wonder how this level of shenanigans could happen. There reason is simple we do not have equal representation.

Statette Representation -Agrarian States usually control land and raw materials, while industrial groups control industry, and trade. The industrial States of the time were very strong because of their control over trade. Therefore, establishment of State boundaries was determined more along the lines of power than reason. If we look at Vermont, New Hampshire, Rhode Island, Connecticut, Delaware, and New Jersey, they all have one thing in common.

They are tiny compared to all the other States.

For this reason I call them statettes. Here is the bad thing. While population determined representation in the House of Representatives, the Senate portion was determined just by being called a state. If these tiny statettes wanted to create laws to increase their power at the expense of the farmer, it was a relatively easy thing to accomplish due to the inappropriate split in representation.

While the House of Representatives should have been determined by population, the Senate should have been

determined by <u>State size</u> rather than NO STANDARD AT
ALL or State sizes should have been regulated.

Even though this representation dilemma was recognized early on, <u>nothing was done about it</u>. The farmers of our nation revolted and were stifled. You might say, "If it was a real problem, it would have caused more unrest." Let's look further.

State Size Should be Controlled-I know some of you are thinking that using State size for Senatorial determination is out of the question especially if we look at Texas and California. My answer is simple. We should use some reasonable criteria of how much area makes a State rather than simply having some idiot stand up and say, "This whole section will be a single state." Let me show this problem with actual people. This chart shows the representation of 5 of the New England States.

State	Pop. [x000]	Senate & House Reps	People [x000] per rep.	Normalize to Vermont
Vt.	600	3	200	1x
Del.	770	3	260	1.3x
R.I.	1000	4	250	1.3x
N.H.	1200	4	300	1.4x
Maine	1200	4	300	1.4x
Total	4770	18	260	1.3x

The chart above shows that the number of people represented by a single congressman elected to one of the New England Statettes is about the same. Unfortunately, for everyone else in the country, this trend does not hold. The representation of the States that rebelled in the 1860s is simply horrid.

State	Pop. [x000]	Senate & House	People [x000] per rep.	Normalize to Vermont
Ala	4400	9	490	2.4x
Ark.	2700	6	450	2.2x
Fla	15200	27	560	2.8x
Tenn.	5200	11	470	2.4x
Va.	7000	13	540	2.7x
N.C.	7800	15	520	2.6x
La.	4500	9	500	2.5x
Ga.	7900	15	527	2.6x
Miss.	2900	6	480	2.3x
S.C.	3900	8	490	2.4x
Tx.	20100	34	590	2.9x
Calif.	32500	55	590	2.9x

If we look at the representation of the "10 southern States that made up the secessionists" and the representation level of California, we find that they are similar as well, but MUCH less representation is provided for All of them compared to the **Statette Masters**. *These 11 States and most of others have only **about 1/3 the representation** level of those select few statettes described above. The sad truth is shown in the table. Just to put in some perspective, I have taken Virginia and put all of the Statettes inside the borders.*

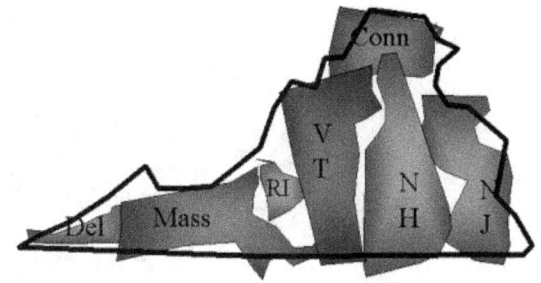

Statettes Foster Greed-Anyway! We had this war and people began getting unbelievably rich as the bought congress started giving away State land to the Railroad industrialists. We have no idea what this means today, but I thought a map would help.

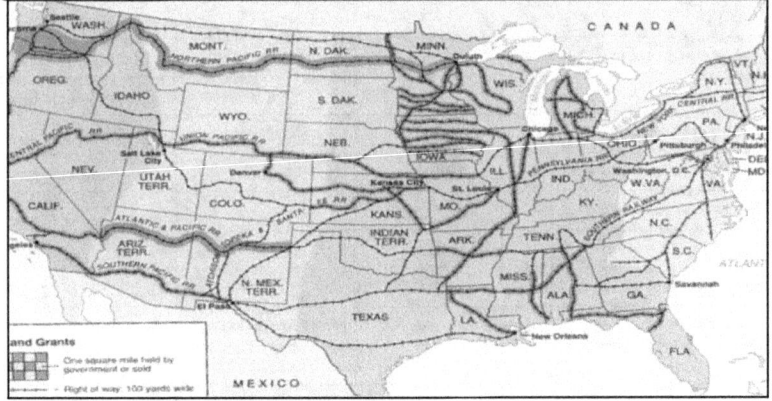

The darkened areas of the map show land given to this select group. To make this more understandable, here is another map of the Nebraska Area. In this case you can see how much land on either side of the darkened lines was GIVEN away. Well over 1/3 of Nebraska [over 7 million acres], and almost all of Minnesota and Iowa. All over the country Railroads owned the land and towns had to buy back the land to be near the railroads.

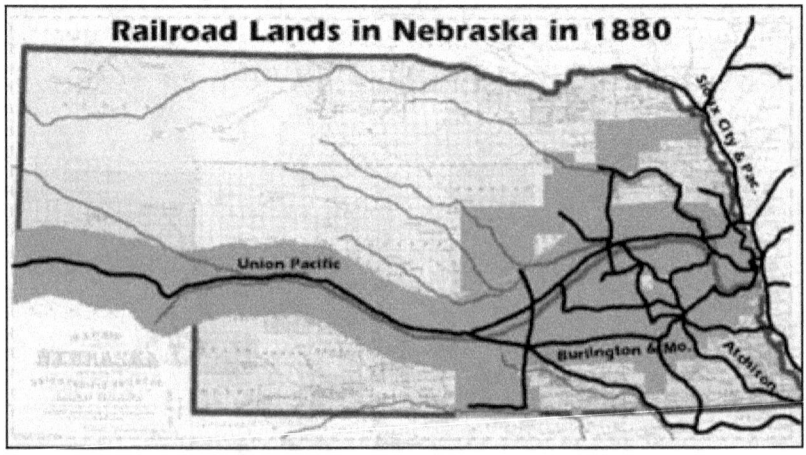

Railroad Lands in Nebraska in 1880

The scam powered by the Statette over representation and greedy congress along with about 30 men and the war was on. Some didn't like the war.

Lincoln Mysterious Prisons-As the war began, a large number of influential people rejected what the people knew to be the President's War. Those who voiced their apprehension disappeared. Rather than discussion these things, here is an excerpt from a New York Magazine that saw Lincoln's reign first hand. He was accused of having little or no trial and isolated confinement for large numbers of people who were against him.

"The Old Guard / Volume 1, Issue 5, May 1863"- *The author of this work was for several months confined in one of Mr. **Lincoln's** bastilles, and was finally let out, as hundreds of others have been, without a trial, and without being informed of the reason of his incarceration. In this book, Mr. Mahony has paid the Administration back with interest, for its criminal assaults upon his liberty. He has tried to kill the country. Instead of sewing him in a leather sack, with a cock, a viper, and an ape, we have allowed him to literally overwhelm us with an army of his official vermin. His cocks and vipers, and apes, swarm upon us like a cloud of locusts.*

Even the citizens of New York understood we had lost our equality in Congress. Here is another article from the Union Magazine "The Old Guard". This is what New Yorkers had to say. *"To Realize how completely the New England school of politicians has seized the Government of the United States, we have only to refer to the following list of the chairmen of all the important committees of the Senate:*

Committee.	Chairman	Where from.
Foreign Relations.	Sumner.	New England.
Finance.	Fessened	New England.
Military Affairs	Wilson.	New England.
Naval Affairs.	Hale.	New England.
Post Offices.	Collemar.	New England.
Pensions.	Foster.	New England.
Claims.	Clark.	New England.
Public Buildings.	Foote.	New England.
Contingent Expenses.	Dixon.	New England.

Practically, the United States Senate might just about as well meet in Boston as in Washington. The same preponderance of Yankee abolitionism is found in the committees of the Lower House. The fifteen millions of people in the Middle and Western States are used as a tail to the New England abolition kite. These shapers of New England thus control over $800,000,000 per annum of the money of the country. The great States of New York, Pennsylvania, and of the West, have comparatively no voice in the management of the finance of the country. Its monetary and political destiny is in the hands of a set of crazy fanatics. If a country thus used and thus abused can survive, either financially or politically, it will be a miracle indeed.

So here is what we have-- 11 States with no representation, 17 States with limited representation and 7 tiny New England Statettes that together were smaller than the single State of Virginia running the country.

With that little bit of Constitutional abuse, let's discuss what happened. As with any society without control over greed, the evil of man will always win out.

Control Greed

Some may wonder if there is anything that can be done about greed. The answer is that while a country cannot survive as an economically thriving socialist or communistic State, it cannot survive long as greed controlled country established under an uncontrolled democracy. The only sustaining government that can thrive for long periods is a republic that controls greed by establishing limits from monopolies and oligopolies. Our country almost was destroyed in the mid-1800s while 33 people became richer than almost anyone because of the unleashed power of greed, monopoly, and abandonment of consciousness. These anti-Americans caused one of our worst wars, raped the American public with catch phrases like manifest destiny, and Industrial Revolution to hide the corruption paid for by freedom to monopolize an industry like medicine governed by a single doctor's union or hiding behind an unrestricted Patent law or smoothed over by special deals between insurance companies and hospitals. The big monopolies of the mid 1800s were in railroads and oil. The following list shows some of the more well-known multi-billionaires who controlled most of the money and Congress in America. Industry controlled the United States during this time and the only reason we survived through the worst of it was the leaving of Americans from cities towards the west. Today we cannot move west so monopolies MUST be controlled with more stringent anti-trust laws, more open pricing, and more pride in America. We must become a Controlled Republic again. I know Bill Gates [number 4 in the list] didn't get his money during this horrible time, but he is an exception.

Rank	Name of Industrialist	Birth/ death dates	Source of wealth	Estate $B
1	John D. Rockefeller	1839-1937	oil	190
25	Henry H. Rogers	1840-1909	oil	25
26	Oliver Hazard Payne	1839-1917	oil	25
38	William Rockefeller	1841-1922	oil	17
2	Andrew Carnegie	1835-1919	steel	101
3	Cornelius Vanderbilt	1794-1877	railroads	96
9	F Weyerhaeuser	1834-1914	railroads	43
10	Jay Gould	1836-1892	railroads	42
20	John Blair	1802-1899	railroads	29
24	Edward H. Harriman	1848-1909	railroads	25
27	Henry Clay Frick	1849-1919	steel	22
28	Collis P. Huntington	1821-1900	railroads	22
33	Mark Hopkins	1813-1878	railroads	20
35	Leland Stanford	1824-1893	railroads	18
37	James J. Hill	1838-1916	railroads	17
5	Andrew W. Mellon	1855-1937	Banking	32
5	Richard B. Mellon	1858-1933	Banking	32
18	Moses Taylor	1806-1882	banking	29
19	Russel Sage	1816-1906	finance	29
23	John P. Morgan	1837-1913	Finance	25
36	Hetty Green	1834-1916	investing	17

- Vanderbilt, Weyerhaeuser, Gould Blair, Harrison, Huntington, Leland Stanford, and James hill all took control of America bribing congress to give away massive amounts of land for Railroad executives. The railroad itself became almost secondary and selling the land to cities and towns that needed access to railroads was even more lucrative.

- John and William Rockefeller, Harry Rogers, and Oliver Payne took control of America selling oil to the Railroads and formed an alliance with them.

- Andrew Carnegie and Henry Frick took control of America selling Steel to the Railroads and formed an alliance with them.

- The Mellon brothers, Moses Taylor, Russel Sage, and J.P. Morgan took control of America financing the Railroads and formed an alliance with them.

It wasn't long before the entire country was OWNED by a very few "Industrialists" while farmers and factory workers had nothing. If we don't control greed somehow, we will be in the same fix as before. I know one could go on and on concerning how greed is breaking down American freedoms just as much as the irresponsible government limiting hope, work, and freedom to all Americans.

Strange Republic Conversion

While I'm on this subject let's go back to an earlier discussion. In the 1870s, massive legislation converted our non-working and broken democracy and turned it into a workable Republic with restrictions on massive companies like Bell Telephone and others. This conversion happened during a time when the men listed previously had raped

Americans clean and somehow found a new set of values. Without the aid of them, America would have succumbed to a horrible fate. I know it sounds stupid that a select group of super rich would destroy their hand in the cookie jar and allow America to survive, but that is exactly what they did. Country pride and fear of its loss pushed them into reducing their control, expanding free enterprise, abolishing the monopoly concept, and the beginning of a huge philanthropic push to help America. Carnegie, Rockefeller, Stewart and others gave away multiple $ Billions to help secure freedom "from" their old ways of complete takeover of the country. By assuring reasonable competition, even when government restriction was hindering some expansion, some freedom, and some entrepreneurial endeavor, the American Republic made its way out of almost certain collapse from the horrors of the Aftermath from our 4th Civil War in the United States.

Uncontrolled Greed Today-The easiest way to determine greed in any nation is to compare the Mean per-capita wealth with the median. I put together the following chart from the 2010 listing of nation wealth of the 32 OEDC Countries of the world. Those with the largest difference have a huge poverty problem and those with similar numbers have a large middle class. Guess where the United States places? As wealth of the country also plays into poverty, I have taken the Wealth figure and divided it by the poverty ratio to give a listing of the countries with the worst poverty positions. Switzerland is worst followed by the USA. While we have the 5th highest mean per-capita wealth Australia, by far, has the strongest middle class. As shown USA "Mean wealth figure" is $301K the Median yearly wages is only $45K showing a huge number in the poverty level.

OEDC country	Mean wealth [$/year]	Poverty %	mean to median	Median wealth [$/Year]	entry wealth level	middle-class Level
Switzerland	512,562	450%	5.34	95,916	1	9
United States	301,140	230%	6.71	44,911	5	23
Norway	380,473	183%	4.10	92,859	3	11
Sweden	299,441	167%	5.68	52,677	6	20
Denmark	255,066	94%	4.42	57,675	9	17
Germany	192,232	66%	3.89	49,370	16	21
Canada	251,034	60%	2.78	90,252	10	12
Austria	203,931	60%	3.55	57,450	15	18
Israel	137,351	60%	3.60	38,164	21	25
Chile	49,032	57%	4.18	11,742	27	31
Mexico	35,872	55%	3.69	9,718	29	32
South Korea	79,475	52%	2.57	30,938	25	26
Czech Rep.	44,975	52%	2.89	15,541	28	29
Portugal	89,074	50%	2.29	38,846	24	24
Poland	26,056	50%	2.86	9,109	33	33
Turkey	25,909	50%	4.86	5,326	34	34
Hungary	28,379	48%	2.02	14,068	31	30
Estonia	33,701	47%	2.14	15,724	30	28
Slovenia	64,067	42%	1.43	44,932	26	22
Slovakia	27,224	42%	1.31	20,740	32	27
Ireland	183,804	42%	2.43	75,573	18	15
Greece	102,971	41%	1.91	53,937	23	19
Netherlands	185,588	38%	2.22	83,631	17	13
New Zealand	182,548	37%	2.38	76,607	19	14
Spain	123,997	36%	1.96	63,306	22	16
France	295,933	29%	2.09	141,850	7	4
Iceland	211,592	29%	2.02	104,733	14	8
UK	243,570	27%	2.18	111,524	11	6
Japan	216,694	27%	1.96	110,294	13	7
Australia	402,578	25%	1.83	219,505	2	1
Luxembourg	315,240	25%	1.72	182,768	4	2
Finland	171,821	25%	1.81	95,095	20	10
Italy	241,383	21%	1.74	138,653	12	5
Belgium	255,573	19%	1.73	148,141	8	3

Some tell you this means we should take from the rich and give to the poor, but that is totally wrong. Instead a republic moderates profit by controlling monopolies, establishing cost controls by world standards, and incentivizes the business owners to get "licence on these restrictions by hiring those desperate for work. The more they help those needing help working, the less restriction.

I know you have heard about this stupid carbon footprint punishment handed out with reguard to putting Americans to work. This is not even close to the type of restrictions I'm talking about. What is needed is the complete restructuring of monopolistic corporate control, similar to the Fascist State we experienced during and after the 4th Civil War into a welfare defeating Republic.

The Sherman anti-trust must be revitalized, the limitation of banks gambling money on the shock market must be reinstated, the student loan debacle must be eliminated. In place of student loans, work programs can be initiated to allow various manufactruers opportunity to reduce taxes, gain secondary government funding, and help the community almost without cost.

We must give Industry Incentive to reduce the slavery of Poverty. The federal governemnt cannot do it directly. I will never work.

What we cannot do is **over tax the rich**. The industries will simply move out of the country and the labor participation rate will kill us just as fast.

Labor Participation Rate

Believe it or not, the federal government wants to hide the number of people that are out of work. It is like shutting your eyes to keep something bad from happening. It is stupid, but elections being won by those least deserving requires this subterfuge to allow political payoffs to industry and executives. While not describing underemployed or those only able to work part-time, there

176

is an indicator that helps us see the true unemployment so we can hopefully do something about it.

What we see is there are now 100 million Americans over the age of 16 that are not working.

The Obama Administration keeps running out the deceit that this is because of all the baby boomers retiring. The fact is that the labor force participation rate for the age group 16 to 24 **is only 55.1%.** That is a reduction of over 10% from 66% during the 1990's. It is also down over 5% (60.8%) from 2005. Sure myopic minimum wage increases are harming the employment of this age group with the least work experience, but that is not the total explanation. The Obama manipulation gets worse because the LPR is lower for the prime working years of 25-54 years old. In 2000 the LPR for this age group was almost 85%. It was down to 83% when the recession started, but has now plummeted to 80.7%. It is clear the baby boomers are not the only source of reduction in the LPR and it is clear there are no new jobs of any consequence. You may wonder why this is such a big deal. The LPR for September 2015 was 62.4%. That is 3.7% less than August, 2005 exactly ten years earlier; if you review the Department of Labor statistics you see virtually unstopped monthly decline in the LPR during the entire Obama Presidency. Even after the last recession was determined to have gone, the LPR has steadily declined another 3.3%. The chart following shows how the number of workers is being reduced as the fake unemployment reduction tries to show a false sense of security.

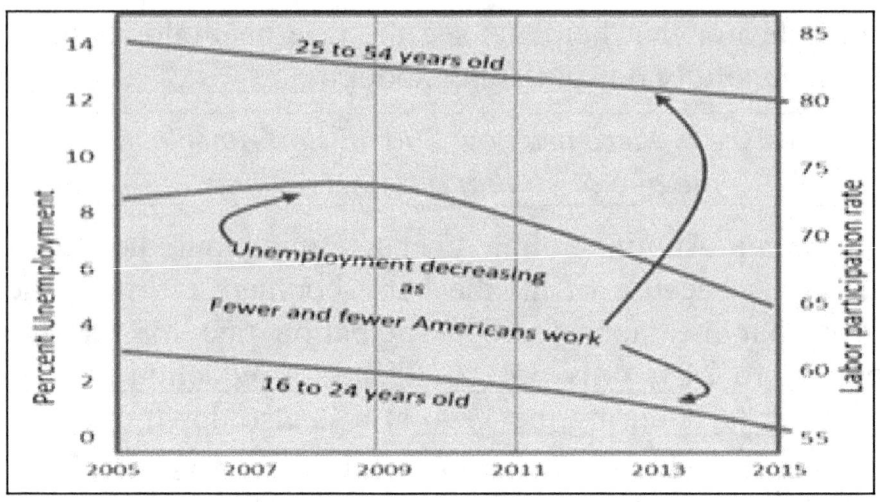

To make these figures worse, we know that more and more seniors are working longer to compensate for inadequate retirement savings. To put a value to the 3.7% figure, at least 12 million more people would be working today if we had the same LPR as ten years ago and remember, this does not include the just barely making it part time and those taking lesser jobs. Instead these 12 million have been added to the subsistence poverty slaves. A cynical person would say the fact that more people are receiving government benefits is the driver behind the reduction in people participating in the labor force. As more become enslaved we come closer to losing our country.

Industry gets so powerful hiring people for less and less that soon, people become enslaved to their work. This is just as bad as being enslaved to the government for subsistence. The reason this happens is something called greed. Don't get me wrong greed is important in building a country, but there still MUST be controls or we get out of control

Democracy and Greed

If a government strongly looks after the rights of the extremely rich Industries owned by a tiny group of extremely people over those of the majority of the citizens, then the society is Fascist. [During the mid to end of the 19th century, a dozen of the wealthiest industrialists controlled the legislative branch of our government. The top <u>0.0005 percent of Americans controlled almost 50 percent of all of the money</u> that was being established.]

Here is a rule of thumb - The wealthiest 0.0005% should not control over 20% of the money or the DEMOCRACY is gone. Another way to say it is that the average wealth of the top 0.0005% should not be more than 100 thousand times that of the average person. In a 300 million person society, that is the top <u>1500.</u> In the 1870s with a population of only 38 million that was less than 200.

We had become a Fascist State which was followed by horrible times for Americans. The only difference in a Communist and Fascist society is if the richest individuals attach themselves to an industry it becomes Fascist [Ultra-conservative] and if it stays as a government entity it is Communist [ultra-socialist]. The only thing the factory workers could do to survive was leave and try to find gold. We can't do that today, so we had better not let it get to this level. So---how did we get fixed? We don't really know, but dozens of these guys one day started giving away their money and allow introduction of law to halt this from ever happening again. The Sherman anti-trust laws established some limits, but it still required the strange "philanthropy" of the previously looting men. We cannot rely on this so we had better do something as we are starting to get to the Fascist level while we are very close to the Communist level at the same times.

The government can go to the other extreme very quickly. If the government strongly looks after the rights of the poor, lazy, under-achieving, or undeserving in violation of the rights of the majority, then the might of the government to control such actions becomes too strong to control. This also stifles business and growth except for business providing protection to the government entity [the military]. This type of society is typically called Socialist. This is started when many poor families are given money not to work. If they try to work, the government typically punishes them by taking away some of their "free" money. The poor families are given more money if they have children and still more if they remain unmarried. Medical needs are typically paid for if an individual is poor, but when they decide to go back to work, the government takes away the medical opportunities. All these things give **power to the government** and are symptoms of its eventual takeover and complete slavery to the government.

Welfare Power-The power is exemplified by government placing strict payment requirements on industry, the entrepreneurial rich and the middle class. This burden quickly reduces productivity and increases the wealth of those inside the government. The loss of productivity hurts the middle class even more than the fascist society. Eventual doom of the society occurs until a strong dictator backed by the military machine arises to force the poor back to work. As can be derived from the above, this type of event is worse than the Fascist society so we need to guard against this one as well.

Here is another rule of thumb - The government entity should control less than 25% of the country's wealth or the DEMOCRACY or Republic is in jeopardy.

Of course this is a very difficult number to determine, but I think we can all agree that Government is too powerful and the highest of the rich are too powerful. The easy answer about how to save America is we must return back to being a Republic. This takes sacrifice, love of country, some moral direction, bringing back the family unit, and especially putting the control of the majority back into play just like the Constitution has explained.

While the above descriptions are way too generalized to be useful, they show that democracy is a fleeting thing ready to be whisked away at a moment's notice. In almost all instances of government control, the super-rich and super poor are targets for special treatment in today's societies so modern societies have both special interest groups controlling portions of the government. We need a new name. A democracy or Republic cannot stand with only the Fascist interests nor can it survive with only Socialist desires. <u>It MUST have 2 strong antagonistic parties to survive.</u> Between 1860 and 1884 we had only one party. Above all else we cannot let that ever happen again.

*A more reasonable term for the modern Republic we need to fashion should be a **controlled Republic.***

Controlled Republic

Fascism can be controlled by strict limits on monopoly, business practice, unionization of the workforce, and regulation without stifling industry. That is exactly what happened in the late 1870s and it could help today if we put the other element in play at or near the same time. So long as there is reason in this style of government things begin to settle out with some restriction in expansion to allow for the General Welfare and pursuit of liberty. The Sherman Anti-trust Act began the Republic-ation of our nation. Monopolies were split up for a time, and intermediate wars helped regulate our country's fixation with self- interest was replaced by a level of patriotism that flowed everywhere. Growth was reestablished, our position as a world power expanded, businesses increased their international base and the strength of our country became well known as the standard of living of Americans during the 1940s and 1950s rose and fell periodically, but always allowed for a new level of **pride in country**. Soon it would all go away as a new term began to push into our country and into the political arena. The words were sweet and included; free love, free expression, protecting the poor, expanding the rights of employees, security for the poor. All this was a smokescreen to communism. At the same time, the freeness filtered down to industries, and industries expanded monopolies, expanded political control, expanded controlled advertising to make citizens "think" they had to have one thing or another [especially in the area of drugs].

It was like having communism and Fascism at the same time.

What Can We Do? - Here is the dilemma we need to control greed without stifling business growth. No matter what is done, trying to control greed will reduce growth a little, but without control soon the country is lost. Here are some things to consider.

1. We cannot tax reasonable profit or companies will leave our country.

2. We cannot over tax those who run corporations or they simply will not hire people or invest in companies.

3. For industries with reasonable competition characteristics concerning how many low end wage people they hire must be strongly pushed.

4. Industries that require substantial research and development for growth provide necessary adjustments for research but insure that US citizens have the lowest price for goods. We cannot allow our government funds to be lost outside our country. [An example is medicine should be lower cost for our citizens than other citizens around the world. Certainly a company could opt out of getting tax advantage for research, prospecting, mining, or building pipelines or transport if they desired to sell outside the US at a lower price, but it would not make sense.

5. Industrial political influence must be controlled- A limit to funding for political interests must be well established.

6. We must limit the amount of money that can be obtained from a suit to a reasonable amount that is not tied to the wealth of an industry or person. After all the payment

should be for the injury or whatever, not as a punishment for a wrong doing. This would only be done by criminal action.

7. Large company G&A tax reductions should be eliminated if a company is not actively providing jobs to limit poverty as addressed earlier.

8. That being said, if there are industries that are monopolistic or Oligopolistic, we must control pricing by comparative adjustment to the world market. This will be very difficult, but if we don't try we will die.

Oligopolies

This is a very important concept as the word monopoly is played with extensively to day. First of all an oligopoly is a group of five or less corporations whose firm concentration ratio is more than 50% (This means they have more than 50% of the market share.). General ways to determine oligopolistic or interactive price and management is the following:

- Low interdependence of corporations or how a group of corporations set price and output.
- High Barriers to entry in an industry, but less than monopoly. [Like hospitals]

Anti-trust Law and Ma Bell

The Sherman Antitrust Laws came along and tried to eliminate monopolies. This was the first start to convert from a democracy that was riddled with greed which was killing America. In one of the best examples of the breakup of a monopoly, the phone giant AT&T was forced to break into a number of local phone companies back in 1982. The breakup was into approximately seven regional bell operating companies (RBOCs) and included Ameritech, Bell Atlantic, BellSouth, NYNEX, Pacific Telesis,

Southwestern Bell and U.S. West. It took more than a decade, but these RBOCs eventually began consolidating. The first mergers started taking place in 1996 Ameritech was eventually acquired by Southwestern Bell in 1999, which changed its name to SBC. Bell Atlantic was bought by GTE 2000 and eventually became known as Verizon. Today, AT&T and Verizon control most of the market and dominate the declining fixed line business as well as the growing mobile phone space. AT&T is looking to acquire T-Mobile to further boost its mobile capabilities and match Verizon, which is currently the market leader. We cannot let corporations to control entire areas needed for survival of Americans or they become enslaved to the Telephone provider.

Antitrust Law and Computer Firms

The dominance of AT&T and Verizon has been matched in the personal computer industry by Microsoft and Intel. At one point referred to as **Wintel**, they respectively controlled the software and microchips that formed the inner workings of nearly every computer manufactured on the planet. This dominance peaked around 2000 and has waned somewhat in recent years, but these two giants still control an **estimated 80% of the market for PCs** today. Microsoft and Intel have faced antitrust accusations regarding their dominance and allegations they used this power to keep competition out from the PC industry. For example, Microsoft had been accused of keeping web browsers other than Internet Explorer off computer desktops, while Intel has also been accused of forcing suppliers to only use its chips and avoid rivals such as AMD. **Both have faced heavy fines in the U.S. and Europe** for trying to exploit their dominance, and both have created some of the wealthiest people in the world at the expense of American Freedom.

Besides the two I mentioned, the oligopolies that are out of control include the following:

- Cable Television Services
- Entertainment Industries Airline Industry
- Mass Media
- Pharmaceuticals
- Hospitals
- Aluminum and Steel
- Oil and Gas
- Auto Industry

Let's look at some of the things that are killing America from these Oligopolies. First up are American Hospitals and Pharmaceutical corporations.

Medical Greed Without Competition

Two that we can quickly realize are the Oligopolies of Hospitals and Pharmaceutical conglomerates. Don't get me wrong, we could pick a number of monopolistic industries, but these are the most abusive so let's investigate how we might help America. By the way do not even believe that because there are 3 or 4 major pharmaceutical companies and a number of seemingly separate hospitals all catering to the will of the AMA [most powerful union in the United States] that these are not Oligopolies. Just try to go to another company to buy some fancy drug only one company designed. Just try to get a hospital action for the same price as the world market dictates. Here is one telling truth drug companies are so ashamed of the cost of an American drug that they provide the same drug to a foreigners for LESS than the country that paid for the research.

If the United States provides tax incentive for research, American citizens MUST gain a reward for the money they spent.

Instead of reason we find the following concerning tax reduction for Hospitals introducing multimillion dollar equipment and multi-million dollar research in exotic drugs.

187

Today, Americans are in trouble. <u>Medical processes and drugs in America cost 2 times [or more]</u> than of the rest of the world and don't believe it is because we have better medicine and a higher level of living. It is only because antitrust laws have failed, and reasonable control over oligopolies has failed.

Better Hospitals?-This is simply not so, in fact, many of those requiring drugs and hospitals are the poorest people in our country. We hide the issue with things like Medicare, Medicaid, and Insurance, but these two Oligopolies will soon destroy us if it continues unrestrained. Somehow there must be given a "restriction of service price" for this almost excusive corporation or labor union of Doctors, Pharmaceuticals, and Hospitals. Certainly, this horror is one that is being hidden by insurance only to be removed when our pain is greatest, but the whole thing is totally opposite the requirement of our government to assure "GENERAL WELFARE" of Americans.

What to Do-There could easily be a comparative pricing of services around the world to establish a level of price control. Don't think of price control as a bad thing. Price control is everywhere. When there is a wide enough assortment of possible sources of a product, the common market will regulate the price, but we found out in the 1860 and 70s that a true democracy [one that would <u>not place restriction</u> on greed] cannot work in an environment we people can become **greedy without competition**. As I mentioned previously this is best noticed in the Medical arena. Let's look at some of the comparisons.

- What you have been told is drug companies need high prices to pay for the huge R&D cost----LIE.

- You were told the USA has the best medicine in the world. ----LIE

- You were told we have more doctors—LIE

- You were told we have more hospital beds for patients. –LIE

- You were told our people are living longer from our high cost medicine.---LIE

- Drug companies currently are getting "normal profits because of the massive research required.---LIE

Everything you thought you knew was fabricated. Here are the figures.

R&D Cost Lie-For this we look at the actual expenses. Pharmaceutical Companies pay between about 10 to 15 percent of their expenses for research, but they use 30 to 40 percent of their incomes for marketing and promotion. Some to think, wait a minute, if we quit the stupid marketing, the price would drop almost in half. One thing to do is eliminate self- prescribing of drugs brought by high cost advertising by not allowing it. To make this worse, these companies pay very little tax claiming the high cost of R&D and inappropriate advertising.

Profit Lie- If you look at total drug company profits in a given year, of every retail dollar sale, drug companies get 75 cents PROFIT. This is not normal profit for anything except for an oligopoly. They record about 16% profit in general as advertising takes a lot and here is a secret. Again, they almost pay no taxes as they show large R&D expenditures. Therefore, the same drug sold in Canada costs 30% less and it is identical.

More available Doctors Lie-There are actually fewer physicians per person than in most other OECD

Organization for Economic Co-operation and Development countries. In 2010, for instance, the U.S. had 2.4 doctors per 1,000 people and the average [not the exception for was he OECD average of 3.1.

More Hospital Bed Lie-The number of hospital beds in the U.S. was 2.6 per 1,000 people in 2009, lower than the OECD average of 3.4 beds.

Better Medicine Lie-Life expectancy in the USA increased by almost nine years between 1960 and 2010. The Average in the OECD countries was 11 and in Japan the increase was 15 years as we fall farther and farther behind in medicine. The average American now lives 78.7 but the world average of 79.8 years shows a horrible statistic.

USA has more ability to pay lie- The chart below shows the truth. The United States is 23rd in median wealth of ALL OEDC countries. This is below the half way level as there are only 34 countries that have made it into this club.

Rating	Country	Net median wealth
1	Australia	$ 219,505
2	Luxembourg	$ 182,768
3	Belgium	$ 148,141
4	France	$ 141,850
5	Italy	$ 138,653
6	United Kingdom	$ 111,524
7	Japan	$ 110,294
8	Iceland	$ 104,733
9	Switzerland	$ 95,916
10	Finland	$ 95,095
11	Norway	$ 92,859
12	Canada	$ 90,252
13	Netherlands	$ 83,631
14	New Zealand	$ 76,607
15	Ireland	$ 75,573
16	Spain	$ 63,306
17	Denmark	$ 57,675
18	Austria	$ 57,450
19	Greece	$ 53,937
20	Sweden	$ 52,677
21	Germany	$ 49,370
22	Slovenia	$ 44,932
23	United States	$ 44,911

We pay about the same as everyone else-Lie-From this level of poverty, we pay 2.5 times as much as the averge OEDC country as depicted below from 2012 data. How in the world can someone say we pay less when out average American salaries are lower than many of the countries in this survey making the difference even higher.

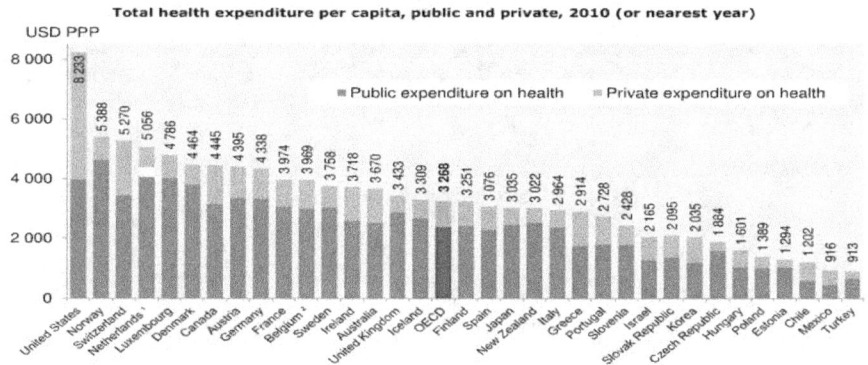

Everyone comes to America for Medicine Lie- The chart following shows which countries are doing the most care per 1000 people on a wide assortment of tasks. In almost all cases we are not the best as more people go outside the USA to have most of these things worked on.

	United States	Rank compared with OECD countries	OECD average
MRI units	31.6 per million population	2nd	12.5 per million population
MRI exams	97.7 per 1 000 population	2nd	46.3 per 1 000 population
CT scanners	40.7 per million population	3rd	22.6 per million population
CT exams	265.0 per 1 000 population	3rd	123.8 per 1 000 population
Tonsillectomy	254.4 per 100 000 population	1st	130.1 per 100 000 population
Coronary bypass	79.0 per 100 000 population	3rd	47.3 per 100 000 population
Knee replacements	226.0 per 100 000 population	1st	121.6 per 100 000 population
Caesarean sections	32.9 per 100 live births	6th	26.1 per 100 live births

Only certain procedures are expensive in USA- LIE- The chart below shows that the United States is the exclusive winner in taking advantage of the population. In all areas noted, Hospitals and Pharmaceutical Companies are raping Americans, hidden by taxes and insurance coverage. We must take control or we will die.

(US dollars, 2007)

Procedures	AUS	CAN	DEU	FIN	FRA	SWE	USA
Appendectomy	5 044	5 004	2 943	3 739	4 558	4 961	7 962
Normal delivery	2 984	2 800	1 789	1 521	2 894	2 591	4 451
Caesarean section	7 092	4 820	3 732	4 808	5 820	6 375	7 449
Coronary angioplasty	7 131	9 277	3 347	5 574	7 027	9 296	14 378
Coronary artery bypass graft	21 698	22 694	14 067	23 468	23 126	21 218	34 358
Hip replacement	15 918	11 983	8 899	10 834	11 162	11 568	17 406
Knee replacement	14 608	9 910	10 011	9 931	12 424	10 348	14 946

Obamacare Lie- The folloiwng comes from the Dept. of HHS and compares governemtn spending to cover the Obamacare fiasco. Using the bottom line we see that in 2014, about 1 billion waas spent and no Pharmesceutical company or Hospital has reduced their profit margins at all.

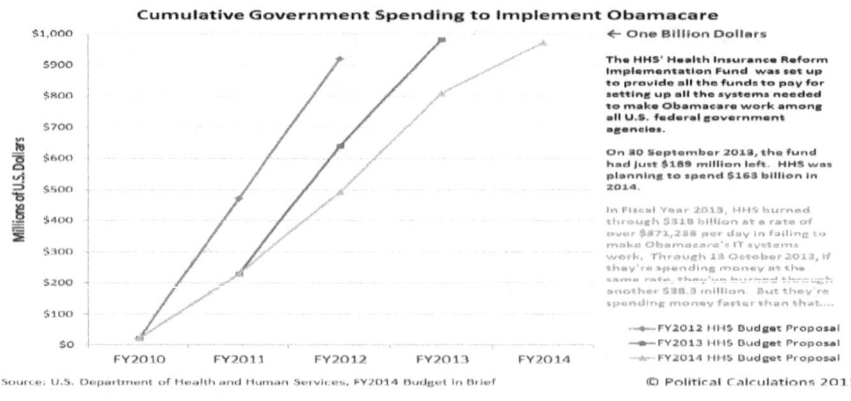

Source: U.S. Department of Health and Human Services, FY2014 Budget in Brief

© Political Calculations 2013

Here is something to consider. Hospitals routinely were not paid as patients without money simply did not pay. Today, insureance is required and the hospital prices have increased rather than decrease. How can a country allow this? The Electric companies have strict profit controls and these other REQUIRED industies must also be controlled. The last chart really is disturbing. It shows that since 1980 our rate of increase has outpaced every single country in this survey for raping the population.

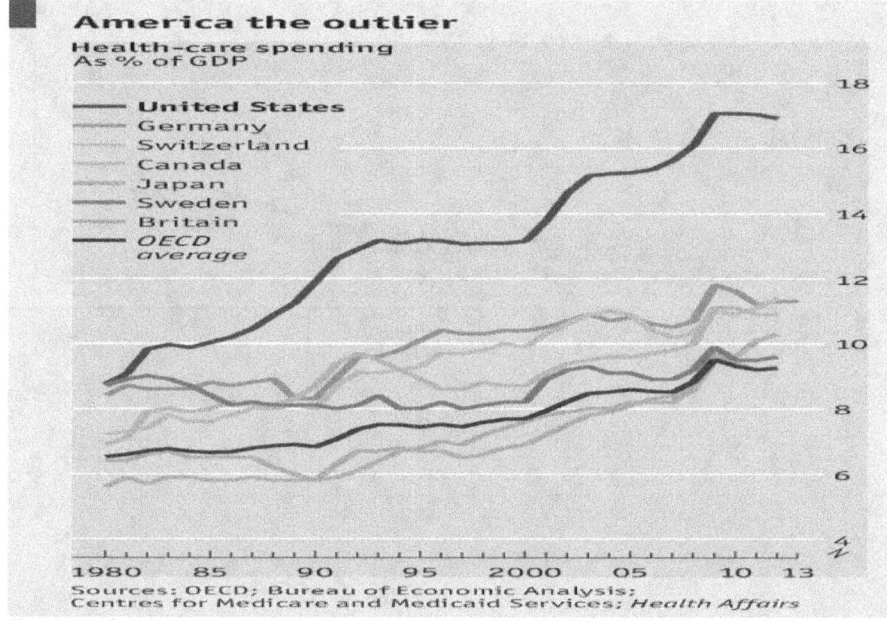

America the outlier
Health-care spending
As % of GDP

United States
Germany
Switzerland
Canada
Japan
Sweden
Britain
OECD average

18
16
14
12
10
8
6

1980   85   90   95   2000   05   10   13

Sources: OECD; Bureau of Economic Analysis;
Centres for Medicare and Medicaid Services; *Health Affairs*

There is no secret that most health costs are directed to older people so the government, rather than doing something about cost control, they made it worse with things like MEDICARE and MEDICAID. These things simply hid the over profit characterisitcs of the medical industies so people would only see the increases as increases in national debt or extra taxes speciiifically made to cover the Oligopolies rather than fixing them. The next chart shows the increased costs for medical things by age groups. If this doesn't show how horrible not placing profit controls on this industry and eliminating many of the Medicaid and Medicare elemnts, I don't know what does. Our average medical costs per year is $7500. Look at most of the other parts of the world.

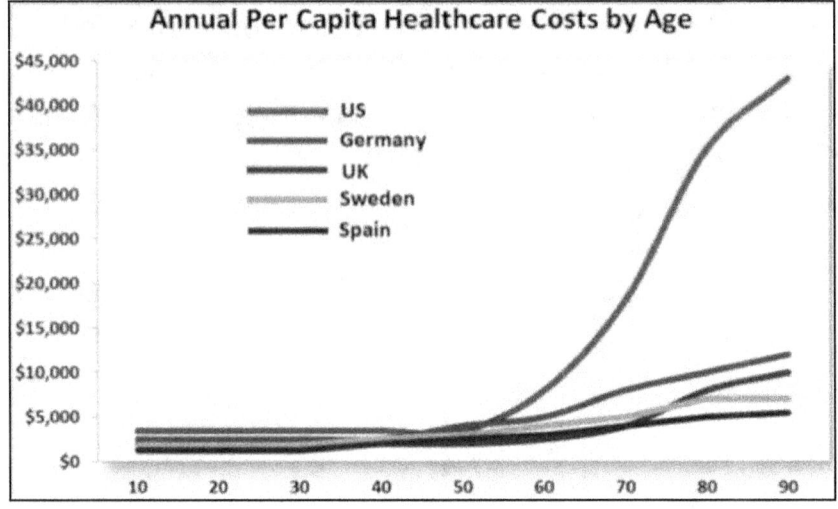

College Greed Without Competition

I know someone is going to say there are a number of colleges so we have competition in this are, but here is the thing. Someone came up with Student loans. As soon as it happened, College prices skyrocketted. It all started back in 1965.

In 1965 the federal government created the program called the Federal Family Education Loan (FFEL) program but it didn't have any meat until 1990 when the federal government backed the loans by placing debt money in storage to pay loans never paid. College jumped all over this and, while most students could never pay off the debts it was a fast way to increase the cost of tuition without losing ANY students. To make this even worse, in 1993, the guarantee program was made worse by having the Federal government in charge of the loans directly.   Let me show you what it did up until 1990 it the yearly increase were less than double the inflation rate.

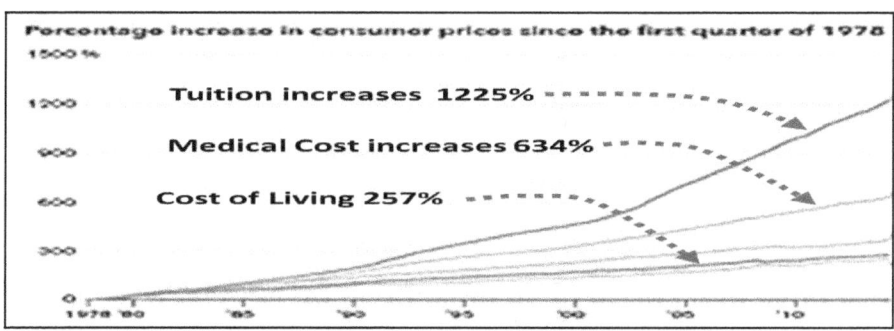

Then political corruption or idiocy broke free to make tuition skyrocket as uncontrolled college profits soared and rates ramped up 5 times as fast as inflation. Now people are saying costs are too high, let the government pay uncontrolled costs to universities rather than halting the whole mess and putting reasonable tuition increase limits on these institutions calculated bake to the 2x increase of 1990 or even earlier.

While all of the necessary controls have to be enacted, a country without country pride will be lost by revolt. Industries will leave; minorities with riot; and all type of things will happen as the pain of restructure must be endured. To sustain our country during the needed change, we need to increase the feeling of nationalism. Certainly having a war is a good way to nationalize the population, but I would hope we would not have to resort to that.

Bring Back Americanism

As I mentioned this is not just a school thing, but it can start there. While there is still a subject called **Civics in our school system**, which is the study of the rights and responsibilities of being a citizen. It has been completely changed from the Americanism versus Communism to something like conservatism is bad because conservatives are mean. I'm not saying Conservativism is the only idea for success in our government, but it is certainly not the devil's abomination. A new form of liberalism is being taught that is more communistic than ever before leading our country to the same failures as other communist nations. Even those professing communism have had to convert to capitalism to survive. In the meantime 51% of the people in our country now are supported by the government without working---all in the name of compassion. The "war on poverty" started with President Johnson and it has been a huge failure as more and more people are out of work; some because they can't work, but many because they lose precious funding if they try to work.

- We have seen making $29000 is better than making $69000

- We know that if we make less than $21,000 during a year and the government gives you money. One penny over and you are out of luck.

- This cannot be good for the country but High School and college discourse on the evils of Liberalism is no longer provided so our poverty levels continue to grow and there seems to be no way out.

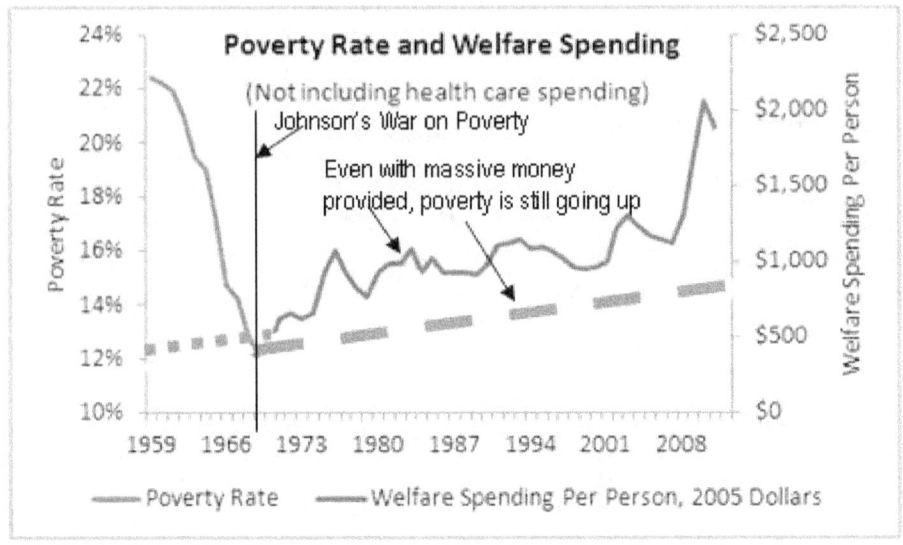

No American Pride

Additionally, those not working do not consider our nation great as they must blame the government on their circumstance. To improve pride in country, we must increase school discussion and understanding of more "republic" style methodologies, get people working and everything gets better. Crime goes down, happiness goes up, government costs go down and our children can have a better education and we bring back pride into America. If there is no patriotism, pride in country above other countries, there will soon be no country. One might ask, "How do we increase patriotism in a land divided by poverty and ethnicity?" The answer is to reduce poverty; reduce hatred of ethnicity, push out any socio-communistic backdrop; Control Greed; and expand the Christian morality of our founding fathers. All are difficult but they can be accomplished if Congress and the President want to go back to the Constitution and actually provide for General Welfare and the pursuit of liberty. Most don't have a desire to save our country, but we do have the power to elect brave individuals that will go against massive parties run by Unions or Massive companies, or the mindset of communism.

Eliminate the Socio-communistic Backdrop-Speaking of communism do you know who Saul Alinsky is? You might remember that Hillary Clinton did her thesis on his great works and you might remember that Barrack Obama wrote about him in his own books praising his endeavors, but if you did not say he was a communist, you would be limited in your answer. Alinsky took the Leninist scheme of world conquest and boiled it down for anyone to understand and initiate. It all is focused on the poor. Stalin called the "*Useful Idiots*". Alinsky had a simple 8 point strategy. I think you will recognize them.

- *Healthcare- Control Healthcare and you control the poor.*
- *Poverty- Increase the poverty level. Poor people are much easier to control and cannot fight if government provides everything for them.*
- *Debt- Increase the national debt to an unsustainable level. Then you can tax more which will increase poverty [by loss of jobs and loss of income].*
- *Gun Control- Remove the ability for people to defend themselves from government to allow easy conversion to a police State.*
- *Welfare- Take control of every aspect of the lives of the poor [by providing food, housing and income]*

- *Education-* *Take control of what people read and listen to and take control of what children learn in school. [So you can divert truth, instill distrust, bash the non-communistic view, limit knowledge of problems, and reduce patriotism.]*
- *Religion-* *Remove God from government and schools. [Without a rudder, all forms of moral attitudes will be diverted and Laissez-faire tolerance to everything will assure the worst will be adopted]*
- *Class Warfare-* *Divide the people into wealthy and poor which will increase discontent and make it easier to tax the wealth of the wealthy to support the poor.*

Halt these things and we will soon be redirected towards a republic. Voltaire said something Appropriate here. He said"

"It is difficult to free fools from the chains they revere."

Reduce Poverty-One thing to do is increase jobs. The second thing to do is increase jobs. The third thing to do is eliminate handouts for not working. Halt the incessant outlay of slavery making payments from the federal government that restrict desire, eliminate ability of work, and eventually consume many Americans into a self-sustaining poverty trumped up by a Government not caring about the poverty brought on by the Welfare State.

Reduce Ethnicity-I know the first thing that comes to mind is have a war. Everyone seems to forget predicessor ethnicity to combat a common demon. That is not recommended. Thomas Jefferson had to say.

"A little rebellion now and then is a good thing. It is a medicine necessary for the sound health of government.

God forbid that we should ever be twenty years without such a rebellion."

What he was talking about was that <u>complacency was the harbinger of failure</u> in a country. Quit allowing division between groups of people.

Increase Patriotism-The more people with secondary loyalties away from our country increase complacency. We must fight to ensure country pride is not replaced by ethnic pride. I discussed the requirement to limit influx of foreign ideas and people, but also we must immerse foreigners into Americanism rather than diversion. One way is to **require American speech** as much as possible. Those wishing to become Americans should not have a difficult test, but it certain should only be given in English and require written test verification. Let me tell you something that is going to make you sick. The Obama administration is ordering the nation's public schools remove this patriotic mindset and establish a haven for those not immersed in our society and illegally residing in our country even when job levels are extremely low and 60% or our American youth are without any job. Schools are being REQUIRED to *"support illegal immigrants, and embrace and value the diversity and cultural backgrounds of the foreigners"*. He is doing his part by making their education paid by American taxpayer-funded education. If a student discloses that he or she is an illegal immigrant school personnel must now *"convey openness, assurance of confidentiality and establish safe spaces. They must also* address fears of deportation and support the academic success of illegal aliens. They are also required to inform them about financial aid options available under the Deferred Action for Childhood Arrivals (DACA) under which 700,000 illegal aliens have been granted benefits and another 1.5 million are eligible with an expected increase of another ½ Million.

Increase our Moral direction- For this let's see what our founding fathers said about this.

Early Americanism/ Christianism

I think we can tell when Americans are at a reasonable point of Americanism by reading about the thoughts of the early founders. What we find is a deep seeded moral direction went parallel to a strong desire to help our country to survive no matter what the cost.

John Adams said- *"Human passions unbridled by morality and religion...would break the strongest cords of our Constitution as a whale goes through a net."*---*"Without religion this world would be something not fit to be mentioned in polite company, I mean Hell."* --- *"Suppose a nation in some distant region should take the Bible for their only Law Book, and every member should regulate his conduct by the precepts there exhibited... What a paradise would this region be?"* --*"We have no government armed with the power capable of contending with human passions, unbridled by morality and true religion. **Our Constitution was made only for a moral and religious people. It is wholly inadequate to the government of any other."***

Thomas Jefferson said-*"Among the most inestimable of our blessings, also, is that... of liberty to worship our Creator in the way we think most agreeable to His will; **a liberty deemed in other countries incompatible with good government and yet proved by our experience to be its best support."*** - *"God who gave us life gave us liberty. And can the liberties of a nation be thought secure when we have removed their only firm basis, a conviction in the minds of*

202

the people that these liberties are a gift of God? Indeed, I tremble for my country when I reflect that God is just; that **His justice cannot sleep forever."** -- "*I am a real Christian, that is to say, a disciple of the doctrines of Jesus. I have little doubt that our whole country will soon be rallied to the unity of our Creator and, I hope, to the pure doctrine of Jesus also.*"

Benjamin Franklin had this to say-"*We have been assured, Sir, in the Sacred Writings, that '**except the Lord build the House, they labor in vain that build it.**' I firmly believe this; and I also believe that **without His concurring aid we shall succeed in this political building no better than the builders of Babel.**"*

Alexander Hamilton said this-"*I have tender reliance on the mercy of the Almighty; through the merits of the Lord Jesus Christ. I am a sinner. I look to Him for mercy; pray for me.*"

Patrick Henry came to his senses and had this to say-"*This is all the inheritance I give to my dear family. The religion of Christ will give them one which will make them rich indeed.*" -- "*There is a just God that presides over the destinies of nations. The battle, sir, is not to the strong alone. Is life so dear or peace so sweet as to be purchased at the price of chains and slavery? Forbid it almighty God. I know not what course others may take, but as for me, **give me liberty, or give me death.**" -- "*It cannot be emphasized too strongly or too often that **this great Nation was founded not by religionists, but by Christians**; not on religious, but on the Gospel of Jesus Christ. For that reason alone, people of other faiths have been afforded freedom of worship here.*"

James Madison stated these words-*"We have staked the whole future of American civilization, not upon the power of government, far from it. **We have staked the future of all our political institutions upon the capacity of mankind for self-government**; upon the capacity of each and all of us to govern ourselves, to control ourselves, to sustain ourselves according to the Ten Commandments of God."*

George Washington stated this-*"It is the duty of all nations to acknowledge THE Providence of Almighty God, to obey His will, to be grateful for His benefits, and to humbly implore His protection and favor." -- "It is impossible to govern the world without God and the Bible. Of all the dispositions and habits that lead to political prosperity, our religion and morality are the indispensable supporters. **Let us with caution indulge the supposition that morality can be maintained without religion**. Reason and experience both **forbid us to expect that our national morality can prevail in exclusion of religious principle**." Bless, O Lord, the whole race of mankind and let the world be filled with the knowledge of thee and thy son, Jesus Christ."*

John Quincy Adams had this to say- *"The highest glory of the American Revolution was this**: it connected in one indissoluble bond the principles of civil government with the principles of Christianity**."*

Let me Say Again

In 1776, approximately 2.5 million people resided in America. More than 99 percent of that population was Christian Protestants. The remaining 1 percent was collectively represented by 20,000 Roman Catholics, 3,000 Jews and other deists. In light of these statistics let's look at America's present-day demographics:

51 percent Protestant, 24 percent Roman Catholic, 3 percent other Christian, 2 percent Jewish, 1 percent Buddhist, 0.5 percent Muslim, 0.5 percent Hindu, 1 percent other religions, and 16 percent no religion and no moral direction whatsoever

It is inescapable that the more non-European immigrants allowed entering and remaining in this country, the less Christian this nation becomes. The more racially mixed and multicultural America becomes, the more religiously pluralistic she becomes, and the more pluralistic she becomes, the less moral direction we have. In 1776, only 1 percent of Americans professed some religion other than Christianity, whereas today, about half of Americans professed a religion other than Christianity as one statement in our Constitution haunts us.

Article 6 of our Constitution- *The Government shall be bound by Oath that no religious test shall ever be required as a qualification to any public trust under the United States*

This means while we know that our country could be jeopardized by less moral religious conditions, we will limit non-Christian persons any office of control in our government provided they are accepted by the majority. As can be gleaned from the words of our founding fathers, this can be a real problem for our success, but it is needed in a free society. That level of freedom is risky. We must instill a strong level of patriotism and with it a strong moral compass to succeed. Without an overseeing control, human debasement, greed, lust, laziness, hate and fear will attack us more every day. Soon we will have no "General Welfare of the American majority who still has the conviction of moral action and moral devotion and American patriotism.

Promote General Welfare

I've been talking about this throughout this book. The main thing to notice is this particular "welfare" is not an individual mandate but a **GENERAL** mandate securing the welfare of the <u>majority of</u> <u>our nation</u>. As the Constitution continues it say **provide for the pursuit of Liberty for OUR posterity**.

One might suggest on one level this could simply say Americans should be assured jobs and elimination of fear that their livelihood will be taken away by government intervention.

Freedom

Unlike the ideals of the Communist and Socialist Manifestos this Constitution was dedicated to freedom, with freedom there is an awful price to pay.

Those who work-eat. *Those who don't work <u>and can</u> don't eat. The "and can" part is only added in a Republic rather than a Democracy. In a free society, even those not able to work would starve, but there must be limits on freedom to secure domestic tranquility so we will investigate that element.*

Freedom is a harsh sentiment. Many American's gambled their comforts in the pursuit of freedom and found unmeasurable hardships, but they were free. Most lived, but some died for their freedom, not by an outside enemy and not by communistic rot taking away their soul, but because of freedom.

Could this Nastiness be What the Constitution says?

The simple answer to that is characterized in what John F Kennedy stated.

It is not what your country can do for you; ***it is what you can do for your country.***

He proclaimed, there <u>are no free tickets</u> here, just security that hard work will not be ignored. Some like this form of government and some like Communism---at least until everyone is so destitute that hunger is common, long lines to find meager items in limited shopping centers, and no one is allowed to worship his God. It is a slow agonizing death.

As soon as Kennedy died, the acting President Johnson quickly got rid of all semblances of Kennedy's statement and through it in the toilet. He rolled out what would be one of the <u>most devastating attempts at destroying the General Welfare</u> every thought about. Called a "War of Poverty", everyone knew it would be a ***war towards poverty***, but few resisted. If we reach back to the time 150 years ago our country was almost lost by something other than Johnson's attempt to produce millions of poverty slaves. The time was the 1860s and 1870s. Instead of destruction by having everyone on government supplied welfare payments, our country was ransacked by uncontrolled big business.

Instead of becoming communistic, our country felt the evils of Fascism.

Given limitless natural resources, an unfettered democracy will always be pushed into Fascism where industries take control of the country.

Fascism felt great at the beginning as industries flourish and terms like Industrial Revolution and Manifest Destiny were heard as the industries took over the country and massive Industrialist clubs formed to expand their profits and control the spiraling distance between the poor and the wealthy spiral. During this time our Constitution was disregarded as multiple billionaires controlled Congress, the Presidency, and the country. Neither worked and neither will work today.

Final Word

I know I have not laid out an easy road. Liberty is hard, Freedom is hard, and survival is hard. If we want a nation that adopts the concept of---

---General Welfare and the Pursuit of Liberty for us and for our Posterity ---

---rather than destruction by Fascism or destruction by Communism, we had better get off our butts and get more active in getting the right people elected and help those special few to make a difference. They will be hit on all sides, but that does not mean they are not helping the majority and the majority is almost always silent. If we stay silent America will die.